THE VICTORIAN MOUNTAINEERS

1 British Mountaineers in the early 1860's

The VICTORIAN MOUNTAINEERS

By

Ronald Clark

London

B. T. BATSFORD LTD

To

P. D. W.-B.

First published, 1953

PRINTED AND BOUND IN GREAT BRITAIN BY JARROLD AND SONS LTD
LONDON AND NORWICH, FOR THE PUBLISHERS
B. T. BATSFORD LTD
4 FITZHARDINGE STREET, PORTMAN SQUARE, LONDON W.1

CONTENTS

ACKNOWLEDGMENT

THE author wishes to thank: T. S. Blakeney, James Reid, Mrs. George Starkey, Doctor Monroe Thorington and Mrs. Winthrop Young, among many others, for help and advice; Doctor Sieber of the Zentralbibliothek, Zürich, for his kind co-operation with the Coolidge material; the Editor of *The Cornhill Magazine* for kind permission to use the material incorporated in an article in that journal; all those people who have lent illustrations, and made available information, which it has been impossible to incorporate in this book; and the late Ashley P. Abraham, for figs. 36–44; the Alpine Club, for figs. 10 and 20; Mrs. Vanessa Bell, for figs. 15 and 16; Captain Neville B. C. Brock, for figs. 24–28; the Centre Alpin de Zermatt, for fig. 5; Mr. Peter Eaton, for fig. 19; Mr. Helmut Gernsheim, for fig. 4; Major-General R. S. Lewis, C.B., O.B.E., for fig. 29; Mr. Hugh Merrick for fig. 34; Mrs. Mary Howard McClintock, for fig. 31; Lieutenant-General E. F. Norton, C.B., D.S.O., M.C., for figs. 3 and 8; *Picture Post* Library, for figs. 1, 2, 6, 7, 17 and 18; Miss Dorothy Pilkington, for figs. 13, 22 and 33; the Royal Geographical Society, for figs. 21 and 45; the Royal Institution, for fig. 11; Mr. C. W. Rubenson, of Oslo, for fig. 35; the Swiss Alpine Club, for fig. 23; Mr. Charles Vaughan, for fig. 30. Fig. 15 is reproduced from a photograph supplied by Messrs. McGibbon and Kee from *Leslie Stephen* by Noel Annan. Thanks are also due to the following publishers for granting their permission to make quotations:

Messrs. Jonathan Cape Ltd., *The Autobiography of a Mountain Climber* by Lord Conway of Allington; Messrs. Longmans Green and Co. Ltd., *Time and Chance* by Doctor Joan Evans, and *Wanderings* by Alfred Wills; Messrs. John Murray Ltd., *Scrambles amongst the Alps* by Edward Whymper; and the *Journal of the Fell and Rock Climbing Club of the English Lake District* for the account of Haskett-Smith's first ascent of the Napes Needle.

LIST OF ILLUSTRATIONS

LIST OF ILLUSTRATIONS

NOTES ON THE ILLUSTRATIONS

FEW photographs of the earlier Victorian mountaineers were ever taken; fewer still have survived the salvage drives of two world wars and the bombings of one. Even when photographs are discovered there is, too often, no means of identifying, beyond all possible doubt, those climbers who are shown.

Even the dates can often be surmised only from the clothes or, more frequently, from the type of alpenstock or ice-axe carried.

In spite of this the following notes on some of the pictures, however incomplete, may be of interest.

The frontispiece, fig. 1, is one of the earliest photographs showing a woman mountaineer. The couple are believed to be Lucy Walker and her brother, Horace Walker, although it has been suggested that her companion might be A. W. Moore.

In fig. 3, J. T. Wills, son of Sir Alfred Wills, is shown seated on the far left. Second and fourth from left are Mrs. Edward Norton (daughter of Sir Alfred) and Edward Norton, mother and father of General E. F. Norton.

In fig. 14, from a drawing by H. G. Willink, is shown the incident when, as described by an eyewitness, ". . . a huge mass of cornice fell, carrying with it the leading guide, Brantschen, and the two *voyageurs*. Almer, who alone remained on *terra firma* . . . leaped a yard backwards, plunged his axe into the snow, and planting himself as firmly as possible, was thus enabled to arrest the fall of the entire party down a precipice of some 2,000 feet."

Fig. 19 is from a photograph taken by W. F. Donkin at the Montanvert in 1882. Davidson's guides are Andreas Jaun (left) and Hans Jaun.

In fig. 22, Christian Almer, most famous of all the Oberland guides, is seen shielding the bottom right-hand end of the ladder, with rope over right shoulder and ice-axe in left hand. Below him, and to his left, with rope over left shoulder, is his son, "young Christian".

In fig. 31, Prince Arthur is seen centre, holding alpenstock. On his left, holding alpenstock, is Major Elphinstone, V.C.; on his right is Colonel Seymour.

In fig. 42 is seen the spring excursion of the Cairngorm Club to the top of Mount Keen on May 5th. Described as the highlight of the 1890 season, the meet attracted a record total of 162 people, including a boy of six, a man of seventy-six and 45 ladies. A formal meeting of the Club was held on the summit.

In fig. 43, Dr. Collier sits at the far left of the centre row with, next to him, Oscar Eckenstein.

In fig. 44 there is shown, from left to right, Ashley P. Abraham, C. Fox, W. J. Williams, O. G. Jones and George D. Abraham.

2 John Ruskin

3 Members of the Wills Family on
Col d'Anterne above the Eagle's Ne

4 Albert Smith

INTRODUCTION

HALF OF THEIR LIVES

I go, Fate drives me, but I leave
Half of my life with you.

ARNOLD

THERE is something a little surprising and slightly indecorous about the fact that the Victorians, the bearded gentlemen from the family albums, provided the first considerable body of mountaineers that the world had ever known.

They were, at first glance, essentially indoor gentlemen. Their portraits were taken against the backcloth rather than the landscape; their clothes were such as to make movement difficult and violent action, one might well imagine from the illustrations which have remained, dangerous if not impossible; their ambitions led to the Albert Hall and the terraced rows of the great towns rather than to the Garden Cities.

Yet it is too often forgotten that the backcloth was almost a necessity of the pre-Leica age, that the Charge of the Light Brigade was led by an officer in corsets, and that the closing decades of the last century were the great years not only of the local debating society, but also of the Natural History Club. The "indoorness" of the period is in fact merely a part of the Victorian façade, a popular erection vigorously strengthened during the last half-century; through its chinks one has seen, too often, only caricatures of the men who wrestled with problems far more difficult than those of today yet who still succeeded in regarding the world "steadily and whole".

The Victorians were not, of course, at all like their caricatures. It is true that they were solid and usually sober; yet they had other qualities, certain inbuilt strengths, which are illuminated most brilliantly of all by the records of the mountaineers among them, that eccentric, colourful galaxy of opposites who formed the Alpine community which grew during the second half of the nineteenth century. These men, almost without exception, were more than mental giants; they were original, enterprising, adventurous, and tough. They were also phenomenal workers.

Just consider what sort of men—and women—they were. Consider Edward Shirley Kennedy, left a fortune by his father at the age of sixteen—he sometimes climbed with his man-servant Fortunatus following as dutifully close behind as he dared—who for a while lived with thieves and garrotters, who tramped with similar companions from London to Brighton, and who was remembered by one persistent question which he voiced more frequently than any other—"Is it right?" Consider Meta Brevoort, the stern new woman of the age, beating the donkey-drivers if they ill-treated their animals, ample both of figure and of dignity, yet singing the "Marseillaise" on the top of Mont Blanc in the days of the Second Empire and then dancing a quadrille with her guides. Consider William Grahame, that ill-starred adventurer who disappeared from the Victorian scene without reason and who was last heard of as a cowboy in the Far West, a man of whom it might truly have been written that:

Change was his mistress, Chance his councillor,
Love could not hold him, Duty forged no chain;
The wide seas and the mountains called to him,
And grey dawns saw his camp-fire in the rain.

Consider Miss Straton, the £4,000-a-year woman who married her guide; or benign C. E. Mathews, organising a six-course meal followed by coffee and liqueurs in the most desolate and ill-equipped of Alpine huts. All these characters—a fair word for them—represented strong forces which were at work in the age which created, in the Alpine world, a microcosm of itself.

For it is almost true to claim that if there had been no Victorian Age there would today be no Alpine Club, none of the hundred mountaineering groups which are scattered through Britain, few of the many thousand volumes of mountain exploration which line the booksellers' shelves.

"All the thought of the age arose out of the circumstances of the age", G. M. Trevelyan has written of the Victorian period. So did mountaineering, the sport which during the 1850's and 1860's—took a relatively small number of the Victorians up most of the hitherto virgin summits of the Alps and enabled them to gain, in a few glorious years of triumph, the laurels which continental travellers had been eyeing for nearly a quarter of a century.

The thoroughness of the record, which in Alpine statistics has the quality of an exhibition catalogue, is typical. Nothing less would have satisfied the exacting standards of the people concerned.

How did it happen? What were the "circumstances of the age" which made the rise of mountaineering so nearly inevitable a century ago?

They were very varied, and the lack, or misplacing, of any one of them might well have meant the failure of the business to blaze up as it did. There had first to be the preparatory work of such people as Forbes, the scientist; of John Ruskin, the man who startled people's minds into thinking about mountains in a new way; of that queer mountain-propagandist, Albert Smith. There had to be a demand for physical knowledge which would drive scientists up above the snowline even though they might not, at first, see much attraction in mountains as such. There had to be a long peaceful period of economic well-being which made such excursions not only desirable but also possible. And there had to be some such range as the Alps, conveniently situated at the end of the carriage roads and only some couple of days distant from London. All these were prerequisites for the development of mountaineering by British climbers during the middle of the Victorian century.

Yet there had to be something more. Strangely enough men do not go to the hills regularly for conquest alone. They may go there first to solve some scientific problem. They may go there to feel for a while the cool keen finger of danger pointing at them. They may even go because it is fashionable to do so. But to climb continuously, season after season, to think of mountains and mountaineering so that the subject becomes half of one's life, to treat the sport thus, as did many climbers during the latter half of the last century—for all this to happen means that the attraction must have some deeper and less material reason behind it.

Many minor reasons can be given in an effort to explain how it was that a few hundred lawyers, doctors, scientists, clergymen and merchants were willing to leave their well-servanted homes for the ragged bivouacs under the colder if more inspiring panoply of the Alpine stars. None of them are completely satisfactory.

The most usual explanation is that the Victorian mountaineers were over-fed with wealth, ease and luxury; they had, runs the argument, to get away from it all for one reason or the other. They were, in a manner of speaking, the real Ivory Tower gentlemen for at least a few weeks every year. Alternatively, they were salving their consciences in the Alps, finding something in the mountain world that might redress the balance of the factory world in which, even if they worked twelve hours a day, they worked under circumstances vastly different from those of their less fortunate employees.

This physical, Marxian, explanation is correct so far as it goes. The material advances of the Victorian years, it is true, not only gave men the craving for hard physical exercise under the sky but also enabled them to reach the Alps with an ease and speed which astonished them.

Yet there is another and more important explanation of the restless mountain-urge which rippled through the Victorian years. It might be the material circumstances of the age which enabled men to climb mountains with a facility never before known; it was something more than this which kept bringing them back year after year.

The Victorians were always asking questions and they climbed, fundamentally, because they wanted their questions answered. They were questions of two sorts and they were asked most frequently by different, and at times diametrically opposed, groups of people. It is no coincidence that scientists and clergymen were so numerous among the early mountaineers.

It was natural that the scientists, the men who wanted physical questions answered in some detail, should be the first who travelled above the snowline with any regularity. After 1815, travel throughout Europe became less difficult, and at the same time science began to push its boundaries far beyond those of the earlier century. The new enquirers began to ask why it was that one began to pant and gasp at a great altitude. Could birds or insects live above the heights at which snow lasted throughout the year? How and why did the glaciers, those white dragons of the eighteenth-century prints, move in just the way that they did move?

Such questions had, of course, been asked before, notably by Saussure, the Genevese whose offer of a reward to be given to the first man to reach the top of Mont Blanc, directly led to its ascent in 1786. There had been other scientific mountaineers who had followed, almost literally, in his footsteps while there had, before the Victorians, been a number of men and women, many of them British, whose mountain travels had been unhampered by any scientific ambitions. Mrs. and Miss Campbell, two of the earliest British women mountain-travellers, had crossed the Col du Géant in the Mont Blanc range in the early 1820's. William Brockedon, the writer and traveller who helped John Murray produce the first edition of his famous handbook to Switzerland, had crossed the Theodule in the Pennines in 1825, and a number of other glacier passes in 1828 and 1829. Francis Walker, who in 1865 took part in the famous first ascent of the Brenva ridge on the south side of Mont Blanc at the age of fifty-seven, crossed the Theodule in the same year as Brockedon; two years later Frederick Slade and Yeats Brown made an enterprising attempt to climb the Jungfrau with nine guides.

Yet all these exploits were isolated examples of *joie de vivre*. They aided only slightly in building up any permanent knowledge of high mountain travel; they had little or no effect beyond a small select circle of personal acquaintances; and they provided relatively little opportunity for what contemporary writers call "the mountain magic" to get to work.

It was only when men began to climb in the mountains regularly rather than spasmodically that the situation was altered. These men were the scientists. For to secure answers to the questions which they had set themselves to solve they *had* to climb regularly. It was necessary for them to be out and about not only in fair weather but in the full blast of the mountain storm; it was necessary for them to camp, to train and hire guides who could carry their delicate instruments with some approach to safety, to build up a technique of travel above the snowline and to produce a demand for better inns below it. The men of science acquired, in order to keep both their scientific wits about them and their lives intact, the first rules of mountain travel.

It is interesting to remember that those who today seek out the last technical secrets of the Himalaya, the Hindu Kush or the Karakoram and who, almost incidentally as it were, resolve in a new way the problems of high Asiatic travel, had their counterparts in pioneers such as Forbes, Tyndall, Bonney, Ramsey, and other scientists who pressed ever more deeply into the Alps during the forties and fifties of the last century.

There are two points to note in connection with these Victorians who went mountaineering to solve their scientific problems, points which have a bearing on the apparently materialist theory of mountaineering-impulse. The first is the large number of scientists who came to study and stayed to worship. Forbes, whose ponderous glacier argument rumbled round the universities for decades, finished by becoming as great a mountain addict as Ruskin (and, it might be said, not such a very different kind of addict). Tyndall, who when it came to writing could rarely disentangle his mountain-worship from the trails of Royal Institution prose, built his "London" house at Hindhead where the mists can summon up the mountain glory as easily as anywhere else in the world, and later made his spiritual home in the little—and almost unbelievably ugly—house at Alp Lusgen. Bonney, whose geological researches took him into the Dauphiné nearly a decade before Whymper went there, was captured not only by the record of the rocks but also by the mountain scene. Ramsay became attached to the mountains of Snowdonia with an affection that was by no means scientific.

The second interesting point is that so many of these scientists, who found in the mountains something that was apparently more than the answers to their scientific conundrums, were in fact geologists. They were, in other words, men whose daily life and thought brought them into full and unavoidable contact with the awful problems posed by the revelations of this science which was then eating so deeply into many men's accepted beliefs. The geologists had done more than any other group of men to undermine man's ancient belief in the certainty of the Universe and in a life everlasting; it would be easy to maintain that in that fact lay the real seed of mountain-worship—when immortality goes, hold fast to the magnificent certainties of mountain-form and mountain-beauty.

Yet the geologists were no more prominent than the clergy, the gentlemen who were doing their best to maintain a belief in the cosmology which the awkward scientists were destroying with an unnerving ease. This apparent paradox of the wolf and the lamb setting out, so to speak, on the same Alpine expedition, is most illuminating. It shows what might have been expected from the circumstances, that they both climbed for very similar reasons.

Perhaps it is not so very surprising. Many of the clergymen of a hundred years ago had become rather too near to God. They understood the codified business of religion down to the last "Amen"; they were supremely confident of their position on the Almighty's right hand; they were able to give the answers so easily that in many cases religion had become more a matter of good cross-indexing than of basic belief. Knowledge had come in at the window and humility had flown out at the door. That was the outward form of affairs; a form in which Sunday prayers at the Bel Alp, the little inn which had been opened on the magnificent vantage-point above the Aletsch glacier in the Oberland, gave a good and well-earned advantage in the life to come over such men as the guides who occasionally lapsed into believing that there were, after all, really "ghosts on the Matterhorn".

The form lacked nothing except the essential mystery. Many Victorian Churchmen realised the fact. And, after the physical circumstances of the age had persuaded them up into the mountains, they found on them some hint of this mystic and needed link between themselves and the unexplained and the inexplicable. What is more, they found that it gave to their mortal work a new and hard proselytising punch.

The geologists were in much the same way. They, too, had begun to explain everything far too satisfactorily. They, too, though in a different way, needed to get out beyond the slick certainties of life to the point where doubt arose. In their case it was not so much a question of religious belief as an intellectual problem posed by expanding knowledge which was the difficulty; yet with them, also, the climbing of difficult mountains restored the balance. The academic as well as the physical and spiritual problems they found gave them back their necessary unknown and made them complete men once again.

Few of these climbers, either scientists or Churchmen, declared openly and boldly to the world the full pungent reasons for their mountaineering. What they did do was to agree that they had ears attuned to the lesser mysteries. Almost without exception, they sought "contact with Nature".

The mountaineers carried this practice of experiencing the rough yet still kindly touch of nature one logical step farther than most of their contemporaries. This was very right, for they felt the artificiality of the picnic at the end of the carriage-drive; they knew not only the limitless suggestions but also the limitations of Box Hill and Hindhead, and of the other physically lesser hills of the world. They realised that to regain something that their age had lost they had to give genuine hostages to fortune; they had, at some period in the process, really to stand alone and battered by the gale with only a fair chance of getting home alive. Nothing less would do.

The Victorian climbers were therefore united in seeing in their mountain adventures something different from a sport, something impinging on their thoughts more significantly than any hobby could ever do, something which was to mould their lives and to fashion out of them such beings that they who climbed mountains were not—in their own opinions at least—as other men.

This deep spiritual satisfaction which they found in the mountains was, it must be admitted, the only thing that did unite them,

Few groups of men joined by a common enthusiasm or belief have had such varied backgrounds, made such different approaches to the minutiae of their sport, drawn such different pleasures from a similar set of circumstances, or fought such bitter and unrelenting disputes in urging their own specific points of view. Outside the bright circle of light cast by the great Alpine disputes they might be tolerant and liberal-minded and forgiving; inside it they were uncommonly like the great teachers, each maintaining that his, alone, was the one route not only up to the gate of the Kingdom of Heaven but also right through it.

It was not surprising that the Victorian mountaineers should have argued. They were too many-sided to agree for long on anything; their interests overflowed into the other fellows' compartments, and they all had particular views of their own—on everything. Many, such as John Ball and Francis Fox Tuckett, combined an amateur interest in science with their love of exploring fresh country; some of the artists, Whymper above all, were among the most enterprising of the great climbers; some of the scientists, notably Tyndall, became not only mountain-worshippers but pioneers in the craft far ahead of their contemporaries.

The reasons that first drove them up into the mountains were as varied and as intermingled as their interests. The professional and business men might first climb for mental relaxation: the scientists might ascend a high peak to analyse the quality of the air; the clergy might, almost by accident, find in the sublimity of the mountain dawn and sunset, either a confirmation or a reassurance of those beliefs which their vocation bade them preach. Yet there were no clear divisions about the matter. Bonney, the geologist, was also a Clerk in Holy Orders and both undertakings are reflected in the reasons which drew him to the mountains. The Rev. Hereford Brooke George, the red-bearded giant who was to become the first editor of the *Alpine Journal*, saw in what he called the climbing spirit both "that love of action for its own sake . . . which has made England the great coloniser of the world" and also a means by which men could see more clearly "that above and beyond all law rises the supreme will of the Almighty lawgiver".

Largely because of this intermingling of ideas and the interlocking of resultant events, it becomes a major problem to judge fairly which group of men exerted the greatest influence on the sport or drew to it the greatest number of adherents. Does the great glacier controversy equal in influence Albert Smith's "Mont Blanc Sideshow" which earned him nearly £30,000? Do either equal the influence of Ruskin's fourth volume of *Modern Painters*? Men not only began climbing for a multiplicity of reasons, once the "circumstances of the age" allowed; they continued to climb for an equally large and varied number of reasons.

These Victorian climbers are slightly surprising in two different ways. They were not all wealthy. And they were astonishingly tough.

Some were, it is true, born with a canteen of silver spoons in their mouths. Others, were like Thomas Atkinson, admitted to the select Alpine Club even though he had been born "of humble origin, became a bricklayer's labourer and quarryman, and later a stonemason and carver". It is too often forgotten that Tyndall, the poor Irishman from County Carlow, first saw the Alps on a student's walking tour which he "got through amazingly cheap"; that Whymper was by no means well-to-do when he first went to the Alps as an engraver for Longman, the book publisher; and that many of the less well-endowed Churchmen who played such a prominent part in Victorian mountaineering only did so through the use of the cheaper *pension* wherever possible and of the packed *diligence*. Even the Coolidges, superficially among the richest of travellers, touring with their caravanserai of Christian Almer, "young Christian", one or more porters and the immortal bitch Tschingel, at times had to cut their travel according to their finances. It was by no means all carriages and champagne.

What is more, when one considers the development of the sport, a development worked up into a great movement by the yeast of a strong spiritual need, one of the most astonishing things is that the Victorians were tough enough to do what they did.

James David Forbes, the scholarly retiring invalid who was in many ways an eighteenth-century gentleman born rather too late, wrote a revealing paragraph late in life when the burden of disease and overwork was already hanging heavily on his shoulders. "He who does not feel his step lighter and his breath freer on the Montanvert and the Wengern Alp, may be classed among the incapables and permitted to retire in peace to paddle his skiff on the Lake of Geneva or to loiter in the salons of Baden Baden", he said.

Forbes reminds one of a letter written many years later by Edward Whymper, that giant whose tragedy loomed like a black shadow behind the Alpine scene for nearly half a century. Whymper was seventy-one at the time, bad-tempered and breathless, an old lion of whom the younger generation was still both respectful and cautious. He was explaining to W. A. B. Coolidge, that pedantic scholar-mountaineer who was intermittently his friend, enemy and—possibly—father-confessor—how he would again visit one of his old Alpine haunts. "When I come, I shall come in the old style", he wrote. "Shall walk up, not order rooms in advance, and take my chance as to finding a room. If none can be had, I shall camp out."

Whymper was, to the end, aggressive, confident, and lonely, all natural traits which had been deepened when, as a man of twenty-five, he had made the first ascent of the reputedly inaccessible Matterhorn and had then watched four of his companions fall to their death during the descent. It was a tragedy from whose effects mountaineering was to recover far more quickly than did Whymper.

Yet in the toughness of his old age he was no exception. Leslie Stephen was not only the editor of the *Dictionary of National Biography* but one of the forty-mile-a-day men. John Ball, editor of the *Alpine Guide*, strode down the scorching Italian valleys bearing his own pack although he was an Englishman who might certainly have been expected to employ porters. Forbes, the invalid, lost his knapsack and crossed the Stelvio on foot with, as kit and food, just what he could stuff into his pockets. Michael Faraday, mountain-traveller as well as scientist, walked from Leukerbad over the Gemmi Pass to Thun, forty-four miles in ten and a half hours and two hours' rest, in spite of illness. The Rev. Wethered (roughly known to some as "Botherhead") once described to Coolidge his methods for keeping fit. "I am thankful to say that I am very fit in health", said this fellow who was the first man to climb the Matterhorn in a day from Zermatt and who was then the Vicar of Hurley. "I put this down largely to the Alps, and to bathing in the Thames every morning before breakfast in residence, winter as well as summer. I am just off to bathe now." The date was October 28, 1910; Wethered's age, seventy years, nine months.

Such men were typical Victorians, many of whom had a toughness which would probably reveal itself surprisingly well on a Commando course, even though the gentlemen concerned would go through the business in stovepipe trousers, keep their hands clean, and ask a few pertinent and probably awkward questions.

The field of their adventures was primitive in a way which it is difficult to imagine today. Adams-Reilly, the amiable Irish gentleman whose lovely map of Mont Blanc carried on the work of Forbes, once wrote of the Alpine world into which Forbes had penetrated in the 1840's, a world not so very different from that which saw the end of the Golden Age. "Legends of air too rarefied to support life, and of avalanches started by the human voice, still lingered among the crags—the 'trailing skirts' of that departed night of superstition which had before peopled them with dragons and chimeras", he said.

The railway came to this shadowy land only in 1844, when the first tracks were laid in Switzerland; there were then only a few miles of them and in 1857, the year in which the Alpine Club was founded, no railways really entered the mountain zone. Deposited at the railway terminus of the lowland belt, the traveller bound for the Alps had for the next stage of the journey the choice of carriage, too dear except for the moderately wealthy, or the packed *diligence*. Even these sources of transport petered out in the mountain zone, with the exception of those few which followed the carriage routes across the great passes into Italy, leaving the mountain aspirant with the choice of travelling on foot or of bargaining personally with the muleteers.

In his inns, the Victorian mountaineer fared little better.

Bonney, writing of the 1860's, says cryptically: "Fresh meat could not be obtained, the bread and wine alike were sour; vermin abounded." Fleas provided an almost inexhaustible supply both of annoyance and of Alpine humour, and one feels at times that old Sémiond, in his remarks to Whymper, had almost the right attitude, and at least the most philosophic one. "I am no different from anyone else", he confidently said of the subject. "I have them."

It was in the Dauphiné that conditions, both of travel and of accommodation, were worst. Here, even at the end of the Golden Age, lay a great area of high virgin country, a land off the main track of Franco-Italian travellings, a land traversed by few roads and those ill-kept for wheeled traffic; a country where even the huts of goitrous peasants were frequently better habitation than the inns; a strange dominion in which the heights of many of the great peaks were still cloaked in an obscurity not so very different from that of the Middle Ages. Even as late as 1870, when Coolidge and his aunt came down from the Aiguilles d'Arves into the Romanche Valley, that frontier of the Dauphiné, they found La Grave, although a lovely place, ablaze with flowers of every hue, almost completely lacking in what would now be called amenities.

> The floor of our room was as black as the ace of spades [wrote Miss Brevoort to her sister], a bag of flour and a sieve in one corner. No means of washing apparent, flowers spread out to dry on the floor, no pillows, sheets like dish-cloths! Will went to bed while his clothes were drying and, concluding it was the best place for him, remained there! We made some tea and had boiled eggs, but neither milk nor butter as the cows are away. Fleas without end!

Throughout most of the Alpine regions, the pioneers were served by maps that were at the worst unreliable and at the best so laughably inadequate that they could not seriously be used. The first explorers of the Dauphiné, who came little more than a decade before Coolidge and his aunt, were forced to use Bourcett's map of 1749–1754; a map drawn only a few years after the days of Scheuchzer who seriously listed the various species of dragons to be found in the Alps.

During these days of mountaineering genesis, the period during which the comfortable homes of Britain were left in search of some new mystic Grail, collecting boxes for cretins, the grotesquely goitrous, still hung in the larger Alpine inns. Men not only spoke, but spoke in careful words, of the giants who dwelt among the thunder of the peaks. Some spirit of the eighteenth century still hung like the gauzy mists of dawn above a world where the safe return of a traveller from the heights was the signal for a Guide-Chef, that autocrat of the guides' association, to prepare specially written testimonials, for the local innkeeper to summon staff for the victory banquet, and for servants to touch off the cannons which still roared out to tell the valley of such a triumphal event.

It was into this remote world of the day before yesterday that the Victorians strode, half conquerors, half pilgrims, walking examples of both the success and the dissatisfaction of their own enormous age.

Chapter One

THE PROPHETS

We are the music-makers,
And we are the dreamers of dreams,
Wandering by lone sea-breakers,
And sitting by desolate streams;
World-losers and world-forsakers,
On whom the pale moon gleams:
Yet we are the movers and shakers
Of the world for ever, it seems.

ARTHUR WILLIAM EDGAR O'SHAUGHNESSY

AT the beginning of the Victorian Age the Swiss had been climbing their own mountains for a number of years. The Meyers who ascended the Jungfrau in 1811 and the Finsteraarhorn the following year, the Hugis, the Studers and the Ulrichs—these are only some of the Swiss who climbed the high peaks of the Alps before the growth of the Victorian mountaineer. Yet each man's achievements remained an isolated series of sparks. The Swiss tinder, unlike the British variety of the 1850's and 1860's, was not the stuff to blaze up. Each individual enthusiast merely glowed for a while in the small circle of his own personal conquests.

Before such isolated episodes could blaze up into a conflagration, three essential requirements had to be met. There had first to be a spiritual preparation, the making of an *apologia* which would enable men to regard mountains neither as areas of danger and terror nor as roseate, pink-and-white paradises where Rousseau-like peasants danced in perpetual good weather. Before mountaineering could reach full stature, the mountains themselves had to be given a new place in the Universe, a place not only where man could walk calmly close to God but where he could, as Frederic Harrison wrote to his daughter, "know nothing and feel nothing, but that he is a marvellous atom in a marvellous world".

Secondly, the technique of mountain travel had to be built up. The best methods of moving on different types of snow and ice, the safety measures to be observed in this virtually unknown world, the peculiar physiological problems that presented themselves—all these had to be enquired into by men entering a world as little known and almost as forbidding as that of the thin blue haze of outer space which awaits the explorers of today.

Thirdly, the existence of this world above the snowline had to be made known to more than a small handful of specialist adventurers.

These tasks were carried out by three men who even in their own day would have made little claim to genuine mountain prowess. Only with difficulty can two of them be classed as "mountaineers", in the contemporary sense of the word. Yet without them the charge built up by the middle of the nineteenth century might possibly have exploded not into mountaineering but into some hitherto unsuspected and possibly less harmless enterprise. These men were John Ruskin, the writer and art critic, James David Forbes, the scientist, and Albert Smith, the playwright, journalist, and creator of the "Mont Blanc" entertainment which he produced in the Egyptian Hall, Piccadilly, complete with Swiss misses, gaudily painted backcloths, and genuine St. Bernard dogs, one of which struck fear into Queen Victoria when it was later presented to the infant Prince of Wales.

The whole mountain world which expanded, set-piece-like, in the 1840's and 1850's, and which grew during the subsequent years of the century, was illuminated by the writings, the sayings, the influence, of John Ruskin, the sheltered, careful, exponent of mountain beauty who was the protected son of a wealthy suburban wine-merchant. It was almost a mixed blessing.

Ruskin was one of the first writers to believe that mountain scenery had something to offer the human race, and as his writings gained influence he expounded the fact with increasing vigour. His belief was summed up early, in the famous fourth volume of *Modern Painters*.

> But loveliness of colour, perfectness of form, endlessness of change, wonderfulness of structure, are precious to all undiseased human minds; and the superiority of the mountains in all these things to the lowland is, I repeat, as measurable as the richness of a painted window matched with a white one, or the wealth of a museum compared with that of a simply furnished chamber. They seem to have been built for the human race, as at once their schools and cathedrals; full of treasures of illuminated manuscript for the scholar, kindly in simple lessons to the worker, quiet in pale cloisters for the thinker, glorious in holiness for the worshipper.

Here, indeed, was an attitude diametrically opposed to that of Master John de Bremble, the medieval monk who after crossing the Great Saint Bernard prayed: "Lord, restore me to my brethren, that I may tell them that they come not to this place of torment." Here, with no mistake, was a man who was producing a good logical reason for going up into the mountains. As Ruskin's influence increased throughout the long Victorian reign, so did he score and underscore the lesson.

Many of the thoughtful mountaineering disciples who slipped through the gate that Ruskin, almost alone, had carefully pushed open for them, have acknowledged how much they owed to this pale-faced young man who was in most ways the antithesis of all mountaineers.

> I owe him a personal debt [wrote Leslie Stephen]. Many people had tried their hands upon Alpine descriptions since Saussure, but Ruskin's chapters seemed to have the freshness of a new revelation. The fourth volume of *Modern Painters* infected me and other members of the Alpine Club with an enthusiasm for which, I hope, we are still grateful.

Douglas Freshfield, himself an equal to Stephen in the Alpine hierarchy, claimed that no one had added so much as Ruskin to the enjoyment of mountain scenery.

It is a little disappointing after all this to learn one disconcerting fact; that although Ruskin travelled through the Alps for a great number of seasons—many of them at the height of mountaineering's Golden Age—and although he had ample leisure and sufficient money, yet he only climbed one mountain, the

10,164-ft. Buet. It is even more disappointing to record that the experience forced him to the conclusion that "the Alps were, on the whole, best seen from below".

This is only the beginning of the case against Ruskin. There is also, on the debit side, the famous jibe about "soaped poles" with which he castigated at least certain types of mountain-climber. Later, he was to write of:

> the extreme vanity of the modern Englishman in making a momentary Stylites of himself on the top of a Horn or an Aiguille, and his occasional confession of a charm in the solitude of the rocks, of which he modifies nevertheless the poignancy with his pocket newspaper, and from the prolongation of which he thankfully escapes to the nearest table-d'hôte.

This attitude condoned if not understood, it is too easy to regard Ruskin as a mountain Plazo-Toro, an Alpine general leading his troops from behind. Most of the evidence does suggest that he failed to climb because he disliked the hardship and was afraid of getting hurt; or, perhaps more charitably, because he did not think worth while the risks of getting hurt which would, in his own inexpert judgement, have to be faced above the snowline. Yet to agree that Ruskin stood merely on the touch-lines of real mountaineering is in no way to belittle his effect. He helped in the essential task of clearing away the medieval undergrowth so that men of good will might regard the mountains "steadily and whole". That he, himself, did not press on regardless with the next job of personally discovering the mountains makes his influence on the Alpine world, so great, so vital, and so lasting, all the more remarkable. Had he appreciated to the full his effectiveness in the primary task, he would no doubt have been satisfied. The second task was not merely beyond him; it was no part of his business.

John Ruskin, born in London of well-to-do parents in 1819, inherited the tradition of slow, well-ordered summer journeys across Europe. He made the first at the age of fourteen, the second

5 Charles Hudson

6 John Ball, first President of the Alpine Club

7 John Tyndall

THE
WILLS
ARMS

two years later, the third at the age of twenty-three, and the fourth at the age of twenty-five.

From the first he appears to have looked on the Alps, as he later wrote of all mountains, as "the beginning and end of all natural scenery". As he travelled through them, year after year, observing, recording, questioning, sketching, enquiring ever more deeply into their geological structure and their purpose in life, Ruskin began to build up in his own mind a picture of the mountains in which they formed a background not merely to one particular set of experiments but to all worthwhile existence. It was this many-sidedness of his approach which was of such importance. For it meant that one could have a legitimate interest in the mountains without being either a naturalist or a geologist.

During the 1840's, in which Ruskin's earlier travels were made, the Alps were still largely the province of the scientific mountain-traveller. Ruskin did not object to this. One of his ambitions was to become President of the Geological Society; he planned many of his rambles with one eye on the strata; he was an inveterate collector of specimens. Yet be believed that a man among mountains should be something more than a mere collector, and he puffed his wrath at those who believed otherwise.

There is a fine satirical passage in his *Chronicles of St. Bernard* which illustrates this early attitude and which might almost have been written by Leslie Stephen three decades later.

In his semi-fictitious description, Ruskin tells how the profession of a young Englishman is proclaimed by his collection of "those worthless and ugly bits of chucky stones which, dignified by the name of 'specimens', become in the eyes of a certain class of people, of such inestimable value".

Together with Ruskin, the young man watches the sunset above the mountains near Courmayeur.

> A few rosy clouds were scattered on the heaven, or wrapped about their bases, but their summits rose pure and glorious, just beginning to get rosy in the afternoon sun and here and there a red peak of bare rock rose up into the blue out of the snowy mantle.
>
> "How beautiful", I said to my companion, "those peaks of rock

rise into the heaven like promontories running out into the deep deep blue of some transparent ocean."

"Ah—yes, brown, limestone—strata vertical, or nearly so, dip eighty-five and a half", replied the geologist.

Such was almost the sacred attitude to mountain travel when Ruskin began to startle the professors into opening their eyes. There are few better portraits of the attitude adopted by at least some of the scientists—although few went so far as this one who made a point of chipping specimens off the nearby gravestones.

Yet it was not the geological approach but the geological approach unallied to anything wider, more humane, or more artistic, that rankled with Ruskin. He could chip and analyse with the best of them, but he saw the mountains as illustrations of something more than the mere physical facts of life that men were then discovering for the first time. It was thus that he could look with bewilderment rather than awe at the Darwinian theses which later in life so wracked his contemporaries. His reaction to the scientific approach to the mountains was in this respect curiously modern. He was at one, in this matter at least, not only with Leslie Stephen—who drove Tyndall to resignation from the Alpine Club by a famous bantering after-dinner speech—but also with such men as Lord Schuster, Winthrop Young, Smythe, Tilman and Shipton.

For Ruskin, the mountains were examples of God's handiwork and in moving among them man could learn to discover himself. This attitude, which permeated almost all that he wrote, is expressed most clearly of all in his verdict on Forbes.

> Many an Alpine traveller, many a busy man of science, volubly represent to us their pleasures in the Alps [he wrote], but I scarcely recognise one who would not willingly see them all ground down into gravel, on the condition of his being the first to exhibit a pebble of it at the Royal Institution. Whereas it may be felt in any single page of Forbes' writing, or de Saussure's, that they love crag and glacier for their own sake's sake; that they question their secrets in reverent and solemn thirst; not at all that they may communicate them at breakfast to the readers of the *Daily News*—and that although there were no news, no institutions, no leading articles, no medals,

no money, and no mob, in the world, these men would still labour and be glad, though all their knowledge was to rest with them at last in the silence of the snows, or only to be taught to peasant children sitting in the shade of the pines.

All Ruskin's influence on man's appreciation of mountains, which developed steadily throughout the latter half of the Victorian era, lies in what he wrote rather than in what he did, for the truth is that he did very little. Yet wherever he travelled he wrote. He wrote copiously, at times pompously, at times magnificently, but across whole oceans of his prose there sails the message that mountains provide fine, uplifting, thought-provoking sights. For nearly half a century Ruskin used this message to erode the slowly disappearing belief that mountain areas were areas of horror and ugliness and danger. For that, all men are perpetually in his debt.

Yet although Ruskin's emphasis on what mountains might mean to man remained constant throughout his whole life, his estimate of how they might best be "used" was a perpetually changing one; changing, it appears, not steadily in one direction or the other as he grew older but from year to year, without apparent rhyme or reason. His reaction to "sporting" mountaineering and the formation of the Alpine Club is typical; essays on *Ruskin and the Mountains* are almost equally divided between those which paint him in avuncular colours and those which list his outbursts against the Club. Much of his disgust that the mountains were being used "as soaped poles in a bear-garden which you set yourselves to climb and slide down again with 'shrieks of delight' " appears to have stemmed from one unfortunate fact; that he was at Chamonix when Albert Smith returned, amid cannon-banging and with great exultation, from his much-publicised ascent of Mont Blanc. Much of his criticism would have been justified had it been aimed—as it well may have been—not at the genuine mountaineers but at their imitators. And it must be remembered that in 1868 Ruskin attended the Winter Dinner of the Alpine Club, joined the Club a year later—his qualification being authorship of the fourth volume of *Modern Painters*—created an excellent impression, and planned writing a paper on Alpine Art for the *Alpine Journal.* Yet the contradiction remains; psychologically he stood always on the edge of the mountains.

He wandered extensively below the snowline. He looked about him with eyes that were more widely open than those of many genuine mountaineers who followed him. And occasionally he burst out with an exultation which suggests those better things which never came. He rushes out into the dawn of St. Jean de Maurienne—seeking, may one imagine, that great, grave, outline of the Aiguille d'Arves?—and records:

> Thank God! I have lost none of my old joy in the Alps. I dressed in three minutes, and rushed out down through the galleried village and up on the cattle path among the dewy rich pasture, the blaze of the snow on every side, the rocks clean against the heaven, and red and steep, and my eyes strangely well able to meet the full blaze of the western pyramid without shrinking. Oh, happy! I shall never forget this morning unless my brains go altogether, and even then the sound of its cattle-bells would ring in them.

Consider what the record implies—the record of a man with his heart set in the right place and a genuine feeling for the heights.

Yet at the not-so-ripe age of fifty-four—when many mountaineers may well expect to be at the height of their power—this same lover of the Alps jumps into battle at Leslie Stephen's suggestion that Whymper had "taught us [i.e. the members of the Alpine Club] for the first time really to see the mountains".

Ruskin came in at this suggestion with all professional hackles fully raised.

> Believe me, gentlemen [he told an Oxford audience], your power of seeing mountains cannot be developed either by your vanity, your curiosity, or your love of muscular exercise. It depends on the cultivation of the instrument of sight itself, and of the sense that causes it. . . .
>
> For, gentlemen, little as you may think it, you can no more see the Alps from the Col du Géant, or the top of the Matterhorn, than the pastoral scenery of Switzerland from the railroad carriage. If you want to see the skeleton of the Alps, you may go to Zermatt

or Chamouni; but if you want to see the body and soul of the Alps, you must stay awhile among the Jura, and in the Bernese Plain; leave alpenstocks to be flourished in each other's faces, and between one another's legs, by Cook's tourists, and try to find some companionship in yourself with yourself; and not to be dependent for your good cheer either on the gossip of the table d'hôte, or the hail-fellow and well met, hearty though it be, of even the pleasantest of celebrated guides.

Here, perhaps, is the clue to Ruskin's failing. For he could only look at alpenstocks and guides with the eyes of ignorance. Although he had opened the door to the Alps, he never had the courage to pass through that door himself. It was partly, of course, the result of his parents' crippling care. It may also have been influenced by the fact that the guide chosen to accompany Ruskin on his Alpine rambles was Joseph Marie Couttet, one of the few survivors of the disastrous accident to Dr. Hamel's party on Mont Blanc in 1820. Couttet no doubt talked about the accident; the incident was fresh enough, and vivid enough, to form the subject of Ruskin's poem "The Avalanche"; and it seems possible that the story of this tragedy so worked itself into the mind of the impressionable Ruskin that almost all high mountain travel appeared to him as overshadowed by almost inevitable death and disaster. Some such abnormal working of the mind is needed to explain his genuine belief that, as he put it, "the real beauty of the Alps is to be seen, and seen only, where all may see it, the child, the cripple, and the man of grey hairs".

The truth is that there was something twisted and something lacking in Ruskin and, as always, the touchstone of the mountains revealed the fact. "All the best views of hills are at the bottom of them", he writes and, immediately, one knows what sort of a man Ruskin is. The tragedy is what he might have been. For what might not have happened had Ruskin escaped early from the hitherings and thitherings of his wretched parents? What might not have happened had he broken out from the careful round of mountain rambles and chanced himself so that he saw the Alps not from without but from within? His eye for mountain form might have led him higher on to the mountains than any other man of his generation; his prose might have thundered in the *Alpine Journal* to good effect.

All this was not to be. And, in spite of the fact, Ruskin still towers as the first, and possibly the greatest, mountain prophet of the age. He made men look at mountains. He made them talk about mountains and think about mountains. He was the man at the lock-gate turning the wheel to let the first trickle of water through. And it is part of his tragedy that he would have agreed with Martin Conway, that epitome of all the later Victorian mountaineers, who once wrote that "each generation makes of the world more or less the kind of place they dream it should be; and each when its day is done is often in a mood to regret the work of its own hands and to praise the conditions that obtained when it was young".

* * *

However well Ruskin might have presented the fine mental case for mountain-appreciation, little would have come of it had not the mechanics of mountain-travel also been investigated in equal detail.

It was James David Forbes, the tall unassuming professor of Edinburgh University, moving through the early Alpine world with the last ruffle of his cuffs in place, who performed this task. He made mountaineering possible, just as Ruskin made it worth while.

Enquiring, courteous, well-to-do, deeply moved by religion, crippled in early life by illness yet retaining until death a genuine love of mountains and mountain-travel, Forbes was in almost every respect the text-book opposite of that later climbing scientist, John Tyndall. He provides, chronologically, the link between the world of Saussure and the world of the Victorian mountaineers. He provides, psychologically, an ideal example of the transformation which so often took place in those scientists who came to the mountains to study and who stayed to worship. And he provides, in dozens of small incidents which stand out from his stern scientific accounts, examples of the wonder and exhilaration which came to men when they first realised the sporting possibilities of the Alps.

Forbes, born in 1809, acquired from his father, who kept a town house in Edinburgh and a country house at Colinton, at least enough money for careful travel; and although always busy, working at new experiments until they finally broke his health, he was aided in his mountain-explorations by the old Scottish University system which crowded the year's work into six months and left the other six in each year free for travel.

His first sight of the mountains came at the age of sixteen when he was taken on the conventional Grand Tour, visiting Innsbruck, Vienna, Rome, Naples, and Chamonix, and precociously sending anonymous papers to the *Edinburgh Philosophical Journal.* The publication was under the editorship of the renowned Sir David Brewster, who printed the papers under the illusion that they must be from some distinguished and original-minded man of science.

On this first visit to the Alps, Forbes was led to the Montanvert, the sunny belvedere above the Mer de Glace, by no less a guide than Cachat le Géant, one of those who had accompanied Saussure on his famous ascent; for Forbes, already cultivating his genius for observing, recording, deducing, it must have been as though good fortune had now given him another link with the master. And, like the master, he decided first to establish himself in life and then to spend a part of each summer on the Continent, touring "not as an amusement but as a serious occupation". He had not long to wait, rocketing into prominence, becoming a Fellow of the Royal Society at the age of twenty-three and being elected to the Chair of Natural Philosophy at Edinburgh the following year. The post was no sinecure. He travelled to London, to Cambridge, to Oxford, to meet other men of science working in the same fields as himself and to discuss with them the various problems on which they were mutually at work. He took lessons in elocution from Mrs. Siddons so that his lecturing might be improved, and he generally swung himself into the busy routine of professorial life. His mountain travels would, he planned, form an essential part of it.

All of them—and they continued until stopped by ill health —were imbued by the same unusual mixture of intellectual observation and emotional enjoyment. In many ways, Forbes, like Arnold later in the century, saw all life "steadily and whole". His philosophy of mountain-travel, his conception of the place which it should occupy both in scientific observation and in the happy life, is illustrated by one passage from his *Travels through the Alps of Savoy*, one of those books which sparked the imagination of the generation which later consolidated the Alpine Club.

> Mere change of scene and active exercise produce fatigue at last, unless the mind have some wholesome employment as well as the body [he wrote]. And most of those who have made the trial will probably regard as amongst the happiest periods of their lives those in which a favourite study has been pursued in the retirement of mountain scenery. Mornings of active exercise, from sunrise till afternoon, and evenings of quiet thought and speculation, with here and there a day interposed of easy society with intelligent travellers, or employed in reducing and digesting the knowledge previously acquired by observation, give the sense of living twice over. Happy the traveller who, content to leave to others the glory of counting the thousands of leagues of earth and ocean they have left behind them, established in some mountain shelter with his books, starts on his first day's walk amongst the Alps in the tranquil morning of a long July day, brushing the early dew before him, and, armed with his staff, makes for the hill-top (begirt with ice or rock as the case might be), when he sees the field of his summer's campaign spread out before him, its wonders, its beauties, and its difficulties, to be explained, to be admired, and to be overcome.

Here is the attitude that Forbes retained throughout life, an attitude significantly different from that of Ruskin who would never have rubbed his nose on the rocks. Scientists of the next generation, men such as Tyndall and Bonney, went one step farther, becoming imbued with the passion for exploration and climbing as a worthwhile endeavour in its own right. Forbes always kept to his earlier attitude. Late in life he regretted that Auguste Balmat, his old guide, was not often employed, and added: "He would still be invaluable to any man with ever so slight a tincture of science, such as would prevent him from scampering from col to peak with an almost insane restlessness."

The first of his mountain journeys was made in 1835 when he

travelled to the Pyrenees to study the geology of the region, visited the Cirque de Gavarnie and the Brèche de Roland, and watched the glacier waters disappearing into the Trou de Toro. Two years later he visited the universities of Bonn, Göttingen, and Berlin, then struck south into Austria, ostensibly to carry out a number of experiments on terrestrial magnetism. Fortuitously, his journey took him into the almost unknown area of the Dolomites where he saw, with amazed eyes, the rocky pinnacles of the Langkofel and the Marmolata groups, and pressed on into a score of tiny hamlets where he was, so far as is known, the first British traveller.

As yet his record had been that of the enterprising mountain-traveller; an interesting one, but not such as to warrant his later fame. It was not until 1839 that he made the two journeys which were to give him a genuine position in the mountain peerage. One was the first complete circuit of Monte Viso; the other an inspection of the Veneon Valley in the Dauphiné Alps which brought him to La Berarde, the first Englishman to reach the little hamlet at the foot of the Ecrins which was later to develop into the centre of Dauphiné mountaineering. In both cases Forbes wrote the first paragraph in a chapter of British mountaineering, the first dealing with attempts on the Viso that ended with Mathews' ascent in 1861, the second with the exploration of the Dauphiné across which the names of Bonney, Moore, Whymper, Tuckett and Coolidge are written so clearly and so large.

It was during these two journeys that Forbes first began to appreciate the mountains not only as an arena in which he might tilt against the scientific unknowns, but also as a source of purely non-scientific wonder. "The scenery is stupendous", he wrote in an enthusiastic account of the Dauphiné, and it was to La Berarde that he returned in 1841.

This time there was no doubt about where his interests lay. Forbes the scientist was still making his exact observations, but Forbes the mountaineer, hiring Joseph Rodier, a guide whose name is woven into the fabric of Dauphiné exploration, was more adventurous. First he crossed the glacier pass of the Col du Says to Valgaudemar; then he returned by the Col du Sellar to

Vallouise, thus linking three main Dauphiné valleys by hitherto uncrossed passes.

Perhaps Forbes felt that he could conscientiously give time to a little "pure" mountaineering in view of the arrangements which he had made for scientific work later in the season. For the previous year, at a meeting of the British Association in Glasgow, he had met Louis Agassiz, the great Swiss geologist whose *Études sur les Glaciers* had concentrated a major part of scientific thought on the problems presented by the Alps. Agassiz had invited Forbes to his famous "Hôtel des Neuchatelois" so that on leaving the Dauphiné in 1841 Forbes made his way to the Oberland, rested at the Grimsel Hospice, and then set out on a five-hour tramp up the Unteraar glacier to Agassiz' encampment. The "Hôtel des Neuchatelois" consisted of a large cave on a rock-island in the middle of the glacier, formed by a huge overhanging block of mica schist, made more weatherproof by a wall of stones, and more comfortable by layers of grass and oilcloth on the rocky floor. It was this solitary spot that Agassiz, helped by porters, guides, and scientific assistants, had turned into the centre of his scientific expeditions of enquiry, and it was here that Forbes spent three weeks during the summer of 1841, occasionally travelling back to the Grimsel Hospice for a few days, but making the "hotel" the centre not only for scientific but also for mountain expeditions.

As in the Dauphiné, he combined work and pleasure, his most important expedition being an ascent of the Jungfrau, the fourth that had taken place and the first British ascent—a climb which presented greater problems than the regular ascent of Mont Blanc, an expedition which Forbes, for some inexplicable reason, never attempted. Forbes enjoyed himself at the "Hôtel des Neuchatelois":

> I here willingly record [he later wrote] that I shall never forget the charm of those savage scenes. The varying effects of sunshine, cloud and storm upon the sky, the mountains and the glacier; the rosy tints of sunset, the cold hues of moonlight, on a scene which included no trace of animation and of which our party were the sole spectators.

Here was a man of whom great things might have been expected; as it was, Forbes' concern with the great glacier controversy continued to limit the time he could devote to mountaineering; and, finally, he was brought down by a series of illnesses from which he never recovered.

The Forbes of the mountaineering years has rarely been described more accurately than by Ruskin, who met him at the Hôtel de la Poste on the Simplon in 1844. The meeting lingered in Ruskin's memory, drove him to the championship of Forbes in the argument which broke out later between Forbes and Tyndall, and may even have influenced Ruskin's early attitude to the mountains. Ruskin was looking through his sketches in the coffee-room of the inn while his mother and wife were demurely at work near by. Forbes, sitting in a corner of the room, was quietly sketching. "Quiet, somewhat severe-looking and pale", was how Ruskin described him. "Our busy fellow-traveller seemed to us taciturn, slightly inaccessible, and even Alpestre, and, as it were, hewn out of mountain flint, in his serene labour", he added.

Forbes was interested in the sketches of so young a man—Ruskin was only twenty-five at the time. Ruskin suggested that Forbes' sketch might be of the Matterhorn—it was, in fact, of the Weisshorn—and all at once the scientist blazed into the mountaineer as he replied. "No—and when once you have seen the Matterhorn, you will never take anything else for it."

Forbes had a feeling for mountains equalled only by his desire to solve the great problems of the glaciers whose structure and movement presented one of the main problems of the physical world into which scientists were enquiring. It was known that glaciers moved, but it was not known *how* they moved. Were they solid bodies which slid down the sides of the mountains as a sledge will slide downhill? Were they viscous bodies which flowed as water flows? Or did they, perhaps, move by a process of regelation, freezing, thawing and then re-freezing? It was to the answers of such questions that Agassiz was seeking an answer on the Unteraar glacier.

Throughout the next two decades scientific enquiry into these problems led to a series of disputes conducted with a ferocity which is slightly astonishing. Men felt strongly about the matter; the disputes split old friendships, created bitterness, and developed into a series of almost religious controversies. John Ball, who was later to become the first President of the Alpine Club, recalls how one day at the Grimsel Hospice he overheard two young men who had travelled from America together, who had studied as friends in Germany, and who were now parting company on the most bitter terms of enmity. "I listened", he says, "and found that the matter of dispute was neither of the common topics—politics or religion—but the theory of the glaciers."

Forbes had realised, early on, that before one could solve many of the glacier problems it was necessary to carry out detailed measurements showing just how much glaciers moved, what portions of them moved at the greatest speed, and at what speed, and from the time of his stay at the "Hôtel des Neuchatelois" he devoted much of his time in the Alps to obtaining such measurements.

He began this work in the summer of 1842, and it is of significance in the story of mountaineering because it helped to raise the status of the Alpine guides by bringing one of them, Auguste Balmat, into the world of scientific travellers as a companion and friend rather than a hewer of wood and drawer of water. Forbes decided to make his measurements on the Mer de Glace above Chamonix, and to help him he hired Balmat, a thoughtful self-educated guide who had the objective enquiring mind of the scientist. Together, the two men spent part of the early summer in driving metal stakes into various parts of the glacier, noting their positions, and finding how far they had moved after so many hours or days. Often they were accompanied by another guide, David Couttet of the Montanvert, and together they formed an interesting trio; Forbes, carefully dressed in a suit of soft chamois leather, long worsted stockings and a pair of double-soled London shoes which had been locally nailed, setting up his instruments on the glacier; Balmat chipping observation marks on the nearby rocks; and Couttet shielding Forbes' instrument from the glare of the sun with a large green umbrella.

The observations proved three important things—that the glaciers moved steadily and not by fits and starts; that they moved by night as well as by day; and that they moved faster in the centre than at the sides. Theories had been formed on all three points, but it needed Forbes, the hard-headed Scotsman, to get to work on the glacier itself and prove the matter once and for all.

Satisfied with his results—and having left Balmat to supervise further observations throughout the winter—he was off again, this time with Professor Studer, the Swiss scientist, first to Arolla and then to Evolena, in both of which places he was probably the first British traveller. He returned to Chamonix by way of Zermatt, staying with the village doctor, for the little hamlet did not have an inn, and then climbing the Riffelberg. It was here that he made his famous drawing of the Matterhorn, almost a geological sketch, which was later so praised by Ruskin in the fourth volume of *Modern Painters*.

In the normal course of his scientific work, Forbes had already travelled more above the snowline than any other Englishman. He was still in the mid-thirties. He appeared to be at the height of his power and on the verge of a genuine mountaineering career. Yet the following year, while travelling through Bonn on his honeymoon, he was struck with fever from the effects of which he never fully recovered. He continued his glacier observations, though he relied more and more on Balmat. He made an enterprising attempt on the Aiguille du Moine with Balmat and David Couttet. In 1851 he travelled to Norway, explored the glaciers, and observed the total eclipse of the sun. Yet the crippling effect of his illness prevented the development of his wanderings into anything approaching high climbing.

In spite of this, Forbes' influence continued to increase. In 1845 he had published his *Travels through the Alps of Savoy*, and for years this was almost a text-book for mountain-travel. Eight years later he published an account of his Norwegian visit and appended to it a note of his wanderings in the Dauphiné—a note which for more than a decade was virtually the only information in English on the district, and throughout the fifties, Forbes kept constantly in touch with the growing band of young men, lawyers, doctors, and gentlemen of leisure, who were taking a purely non-scientific interest in the Alps.

In 1853 he invited Balmat to visit him at his home in England, and subsequently introduced him to Wills, thus being the godfather of that long association which culminated in Wills' famous ascent of the Wetterhorn and ended with Balmat's death in Wills' chalet, The Eagle's Nest, in the Valley of Sixt. He encouraged Adams-Reilly in his great project of mapping Mont Blanc, and played a significant part in having the map published by the Alpine Club of which he was, in 1859, made the first honorary member.

Forbes died in 1868, worn out by illness and work, and rather wondering, one may imagine, at the implications of the Matterhorn disaster, whose sole English survivor, Edward Whymper, had explained to him in the Birmingham house where the formation of the Alpine Club had first been formally discussed, just how the dreadful accident had taken place.

Forbes never bowed to the new non-scientific reasons for mountaineering which grew up during his later years. He never developed into a mountaineer as did some of the later scientists such as Tyndall and Bonney. Yet during the later period of his life he was, as was said of Coolidge, "the great master". He had, after all, sensed the attraction of the great mountains before Edward Whymper had been born. He had, moreover, discovered by quiet observation how one could travel among them in relative safety.

Neither Ruskin's revelation of the mountain glory nor Forbes' careful enquiring journeys would have had much effect on the Victorian public had it not been for the activities of a third man. Both Ruskin and Forbes spoke to the informed, discerning, one-thousandth of the population; few even among this small minority had any real knowledge of mountains and for the middle classes, let alone for the vast belly-and-body masses, the Alps and their names were not even symbols but queer words which meant little more than unusual sounds used by men back from abroad.

Someone very different from either Forbes or Ruskin was needed before any knowledge of mountains or mountaineering could, like rain on the earth, filter down deeply and yet more deeply among Victoria's subjects so that eventually even the most inarticulate had heard of at least one mountain.

Albert Smith, "the man of Mont Blanc", was cut for the job. He was different, harder, harsher, than either Ruskin or Forbes. His early background was that of the small surgeon's practice built up by his father in a sleepy Surrey town; his later experience that of a rather Bohemian playwright and author who was rarely worried by such *bourgeois* matters as solvency.

Smith's story is misleadingly simple. He was born in Chertsey in 1816, received as a child a copy of *The Peasants of Chamouni*, a book which described the accident to Dr. Hamel's party on Mont Blanc, in 1820, and subsequently followed the news of each new ascent of the mountain with an almost pathological interest. The idea of climbing Mont Blanc obsessed him even though he knew little or nothing about any other mountain in the Alps. He studied medicine in Paris, made a brave, hitch-hiking, roister-doister journey to Chamonix—where he volunteered, unsuccessfully, as a porter willing to accompany any party setting out for the summit—and returned to London where the profession of doctoring gradually left him and where he turned to writing as an alternative love.

As a contributor to *Punch*, an author of light plays, as dramatic critic to the *Illustrated London News* and joint editor of a short-lived magazine, *The Man in the Moon*, Smith trundled steadily up the ladder in his new profession in a deft but slightly haphazard way. In 1849 he visited the Middle East and returned to London where in 1851 he gave his first public entertainment, "The Overland Mail".

The same year, Smith set out for Mont Blanc, a venture the thought of which had nattered away at him for more than a decade. Throughout the rough-and-tumble of authorship he had retained much of the genuine mountain enthusiasm which had driven him across France as a younger man with only a few pounds in his pocket so that he might look at Mont Blanc and chance his arm at climbing her. He had gone back to Chamonix whenever the chance offered, spending a week or so with his friends the Tairraz at the Hôtel de Londres; kept from making the ascent of Mont Blanc, one feels, more by lack of finance than by lack of courage.

Now, as a result of the success of "The Overland Mail" he had money and leisure; both would be contributed to the ascent of Mont Blanc. Smith was in almost every respect a totally different sort of man from those who were about to create the sport of mountaineering. It was not merely that he was different from, and slightly disliked by, his contemporaries—Douglas Jerrold claimed that his initials represented merely two-thirds of the truth, while Dickens resigned from the Garrick Club when Smith was elected—for in this he was comparable to many of the most famous Victorian mountaineers, men of singular opinions, stubborn will, and angry words. Smith was something more, something that might have been considered quite inexcusable. He was rather showy, and his profession, his enthusiasm, and his ignorance brought him at times perilously near the edge of vulgarity.

Sala's description of him paints a man who in most details was a strange contrast to the future elders of the Alpine Club.

> I can recall him [writes Sala] as a sturdy-looking, broad-shouldered, short-necked man, with grey eyes, and flowing locks of light brown, and large side-whiskers; later in life he wore a beard; and, on the whole, he bore a most striking resemblance to Mr. Comyns Carr. His voice was a high treble; his study was like a curiosity shop; although the "curios" were not highly remarkable from the standpoint of high art, and were not very antique. Littered about the room, which was on the ground floor, were piles of French novels, in yellow paper covers, dolls, caricatures, toys of every conceivable kind, a *debardeuse* silk shirt, crimson sash, and velvet trousers, the white linen raiment of a Pierrot, cakes of soap from Vienna, made in the simultude of fruit, iron jewellery from Berlin of the historic "*Ich gab Gold für Essen*" pattern, miniature Swiss chalets, porcelain and meerschaum pipes—although Albert was no smoker—and the model of a French *diligence*.

He was also, adds Sala, one of the kindest and cheeriest of mankind. He might have added that Smith was also one of the most casual—on his wedding-day he was found, at the hour planned for the ceremony, quietly reading a paper at home, a position from which he was dragged away by the officiating clergyman.

Yet there can be no doubt that Albert Smith, when he set out for Mont Blanc, had a genuine enthusiasm for the adventure, even though he knew that with any luck the ascent would provide the material for some public performance. He set out in the right spirit.

> I found my old knapsack in a store-room [he writes], and I beat out the moths and spiders, and filled it as of old, and on the first of August, 1851, I left London Bridge in the mail-train of the South-Eastern Railway, with my Lord Mayor and other distinguished members of the corporation, who were going to the *fêtes* at Paris in honour of the Exhibition, and who, not having a knapsack under their seat, lost all their luggage, as is no doubt chronicled in the City archives.

At Chamonix he was joined by three men, Francis Philips, the Hon. William Edward Sackville-West, and Charles G. Floyd, all of whom were glad to join Mr. Smith in his ascent once they learned his identity. The first two were to become, like Smith himself, members of the Alpine Club solely on the strength of their ascent of Mont Blanc.

After a day's waiting for good weather, the party set off, one of the largest and most unwieldy parties ever to straggle out from Chamonix. There was Smith and his three companions, a total of sixteen guides, and about a score of porters and other volunteers who were accompanying the party varying distances up the mountain.

The table of provisions provides an interesting comparison with the contemporary meal-in-a-biscuit school, and an indication that the Victorians set about climbing much as Wellington—"first a full belly and then at 'em"—set about war.

Here are the provisions which added 456 francs, or roughly £45, to the cost of Smith's expedition:

60 bottles of Vin Ordinaire
6 bottles of Bordeaux
10 bottles of St. George
15 bottles of St. Jean
3 bottles of Cognac
1 bottle of Syrup of Raspberries
6 bottles of Lemonade
2 bottles of Champagne
20 loaves
10 small cheeses
6 packets of chocolate
6 packets of sugar
4 packets of prunes
4 packets of raisins
2 packets of salt
4 wax candles
6 lemons
4 legs of mutton
4 shoulders of mutton
6 pieces of veal
1 piece of beef
11 large fowls
35 small fowls

The ascent, made at a cost of nearly £60 for each of the four travellers, was unremarkable. There was a bivouac on the Grands Mulets, a fine view from the summit, a safe descent, and a triumphal entry into the village of Chamonix with cannons firing, the whole population a-flutter with handkerchiefs in the main street, and a festive table in the courtyard of the Hôtel de Londres, dressed with bouquets and champagne bottles.

The ascent, the thirty-seventh of the mountain and the first to be made by any future member of the Alpine Club, was not without its critics, partly due to a particularly boisterous party held in Chamonix by Sir Robert Peel.

> Saussure's observations and his reflections on Mont Blanc live in his poetical philosophy [said the *Daily News*]. Those of Mr. Albert Smith will be most appropriately accorded in a tissue of indifferent puns and stale fast witticisms, with an incessant straining after smartness. The aimless scramble of the four pedestrians to the top of Mont Blanc, with the accompaniment of Sir Robert Peel's orgies at the bottom, will not go far to redeem the somewhat equivocal reputation of the herd of English tourists in Switzerland, for a mindless and rather vulgar redundance of animal spirits.

Much the same criticism was to be levelled against both Smith's description of the ascent, which forms the concluding chapters of his *The Story of Mont Blanc*, and "The Ascent of Mont Blanc", the entertainment which he subsequently produced at the Egyptian Hall in Piccadilly. Both were a curious mixture of gauche sensation, in which every incident was over-dramatised, and a certain rather naïve innocence. Both survived the criticisms.

"The Ascent of Mont Blanc", a display in which Smith personally described a series of dioramic views drawn by William Beverley, and in which the whole journey from London to the summit of Mont Blanc was interlarded with historical, topographical, and various less serious allusions, opened on March 15, 1852. Even after the first performance, Smith appears to have been uncertain as to its financial success. He need not have worried.

"Mount Blanc" ran until two years before Smith's death in 1860. Only three months after its first performance, the Prince Consort, the Prince of Wales—the future Edward VII—and Prince Alfred, attended a special private morning performance of the show. Two years later a special performance was given before the Queen and the Prince Consort at Osborne, Smith afterwards being presented with a diamond scarf-pin by the Queen; and, yet another two years afterwards, a third Command performance was given, this time at Windsor before the Court and King Leopold I of Belgium. The show, for such it was, played to packed houses, making Smith not only financially but in reputation, so that for a whole segment of the population he became "the man of Mont Blanc".

"The Game of Mont Blanc", complete with rules and counters, and approximating roughly to an Alpine snakes-and-ladders, was sold by the thousand while the music which drummed through the mid-1850's included, as a direct result of Albert Smith's efforts, the "Mont Blanc Quadrille" and the "Chamonix Polka". St. Bernard dogs were brought to London by François Favret, one of Smith's guides, and one of the animals presented to the Queen. Swiss misses, Swiss costumes, and all the attributes of a carefully planned advertising campaign jollied up enthusiasm while Smith was filling the Egyptian Hall. Throughout it all he returned to Chamonix almost every year, being fêted not only as a good fellow but also as a public benefactor. In 1853 he was invited to the ceremonial opening of the first hut on Mont Blanc; four years later he was invited to the village so that he might conduct the Prince of Wales, then making his first visit to Switzerland, on a tour of the Glacier des Bossons. Almost everything that he did had some publicity value for the show which is claimed to have brought him £30,000, and which certainly accounted for most of the £18,000 which he left when he died.

There can, from the safe, secure, educated viewpoint of the Victorian mountaineers, have been few things more likely to bring Alpine climbing into disrepute than Albert Smith and his rather ostentatious showmanship. Yet in spite of it Albert Smith received, and accepted, an invitation to become an original member of the Alpine Club—revealing in his reply, incidentally, that he and John Auldjo, who had climbed Mont Blanc in 1827, had once contemplated forming an Alpine club. Even such a grim, behind-the-stockades figure as Douglas Freshfield, who saw Smith's show at the age of nine, admired the man of Mont Blanc and later wrote of him that:

> He came forward just at the psychological moment when railways across France had brought the Alps within the Englishman's long vacation. And, strange to say, he had a genuine passion for Mont Blanc, which fortune or rather his own enthusiasm enabled him to put to profit.

Whatever failings Smith may have had, he did two things. He

encouraged men to visit Chamonix, and not a few of those who did so took the next step and climbed Mont Blanc. Secondly, and more important, Smith revealed to scores of young men that there existed a field for adventure which they had never before suspected. Most of his audience naturally consisted of men and women who would never visit the Alps, let alone climb them. Yet among the crowd there was more than one youngster who looked, through the slightly distorting eyes of Smith as through magic casements. On nearer acquaintance he might revise his opinions of what he saw. The mountains might appear to him in a light rather different from that of the gas-lit Egyptian Hall with its girls in national costume, its fancy programmes, and its Barnum-and-Bailey atmosphere. Yet without Albert Smith he would never have felt like "that watcher of the skies when a new planet swims into his ken". His eagle eyes would never have discerned that new world waiting to be conquered which lay beyond the bluster and rumbustious exaggerations of Albert Smith.

Smith helped to convert many young men to mountaineering and for this he was forgiven much. Yet there is another reason for the influence which he exercised over the most unexpected of the Victorians. This is his sincerity. He really loved the Alps, and the more discerning among his audiences sensed, even if they did not know, that he had not gone to Chamonix entirely with the idea of making money.

It is a little too easy to laugh at Smith's sensational descriptions. It is difficult to agree that, as he says of the Mur de la Cote: "Should the foot slip, or the baton give way, there is no chance for life—you would glide like lightning from one frozen crag to another and finally be dashed to pieces, hundreds and hundreds of feet below in the horrible depths of the glacier." Yet even a few years later Alfred Wills, that sober, experienced and careful climber who was to become President of the Alpine Club, could say, of the summit of the Wetterhorn: "I was almost appalled by our position." Neither words nor situation are exactly comparable, but it is possible to believe that Smith was merely putting into the language of his public much the same thoughts that fluttered at times across the minds of many early climbers as they pioneered their ways up what was later to become "an easy day for a lady".

Yet the real reason for Albert Smith's extravagant terms, so out of keeping both with the other mountain language of the time and with what he appears genuinely to have felt, was a rather different one.

Smith saw the mountains, epitomised by Mont Blanc, not clearly as Forbes had seen them, not with the eyes of genius through which Ruskin had looked at them, but through a luminous golden haze of unreality. His writing was in one way queerly comparable with that of the modern rock-climbing writers who go to the other extreme with carefully stressed understatement. Both reject the idea that the common mass can stand, as it were, on "the edge of all things". For Albert Smith, Mont Blanc was the Promised Land. Round it he built his own imaginative fortifications, making it not only for him but for all those who might crowd into his display, a distant, virtually inaccessible place, a sanctuary about which one might inform the crowd but about which it would be unwise to let slip too much factual information.

In spite of the cannons of Chamonix, in spite of Ruskin's disgust, the man of Mont Blanc was much nearer in spirit both to Forbes and to the "Don Quixote of Denmark Hill", than any of the three ever imagined. All would have been gravely offended by the idea that Mont Blanc could be ascended without guides as it was by Kennedy's party in 1855. All would have ridiculed the idea that it could ever be climbed alone, as it was by Frederick Morshead in 1864.

All had to make their own individual contributions before there was much hope of mountain-climbing developing into a serious and significant method of employing one's time.

Chapter Two

PIONEERS, O PIONEERS

And greatness is the vision, not the deed.
Greatness is to be one with the vision, and ensue it,
Greatness is suffering, greatness a long need,
And distant bugles crying faintly through it,
"Lights out! Lights out!"
Greatness is to hear the bugles and not to doubt.

HUMBERT WOLFE

THE mountain world whose existence was revealed in the forties and fifties was investigated by men who were explorers rather than mountaineers. They were mainly interested in treading into those places of which men had no knowledge; only by chance did the one area for their discoveries remaining in Europe lie above the snowline. These explorers had a virgin innocence of the first principles of mountaineering; they let their ropes be *held* by guides, they knew nothing of breaking strains, and they built up their principles of snow-craft almost as they went along, largely by trial and error. Only later, as the Golden Age continued during the later 1850's, did the glories of the mountain world, as such, usurp the prime glory of discovery; only then, as a result of mutual intercourse and the exchange of experience, did the happy few develop the craft of mountaineering.

It is not easy to understand the lustre of the unknown that hung about the Alps little more than a hundred years ago.

When Queen Victoria came to the throne, the summit of Mont Blanc had been reached, as a most exceptional effort, only half a century previously and only some thirty men, other than the guides, had stood upon its summit since that memorable event. The Jungfrau and the Finsteraarhorn had, it is true, been climbed by those redoubtable Swiss brothers, the Meyers. Two of the lower peaks of Monte Rosa had been climbed, although the summit had so far escaped the conquerors. There were a number of passes across the Alps, as there had been for hundreds of years, but in between there lay a country, running from the Mediterranean to the peaks of Austria, which was as little known to most Englishmen as far Cathay. For the Victorian mountaineers, the Alps, only recently depopulated of dragons yet lying in a great crescent only some 400 miles from their comfortable firesides, had much the same significance as the thin blue haze of outer space has for the adventurers of today.

Toward the western end of this crescent lay Mont Blanc, the most famous as well as the highest mountain in the Alps. Near its foot lay Chamonix, later to become the centre for ascents not only of Mont Blanc but of a whole galaxy of fine peaks around it such as the Aiguille Verte, Mont Mallet, and Mont Dolent. To the east lay the Pennine Alps with Monte Rosa, one of the few mountains in the range whose ascent had been frequently attempted, and whose lower summits had been reached. Near by lay such peaks as the Weisshorn, the Dent Blanche, the Grand Combin, the Matterhorn, and a score of minor summits, many of them easily accessible from the little hamlet of Zermatt.

To the north and north-east, across the deep trough of the Rhône Valley, lay the Bernese Oberland with the great peaks of the Jungfrau, Mönch, and Eiger so plainly visible from the northern plain of Switzerland; with the Wetterhorn, rising almost from the outskirts of the village of Grindelwald; and, deeper in the group, among a tangle of glaciers that were the longest in the whole of the Alps, such mountains as the Schreckhorn and the Finsteraarhorn. Farther east stretched the Lepontine and the Bernina Alps as well as the Dolomites and numerous smaller and lower groups.

In the far south-west, beyond the Graian Alps, lay the Dauphiné with its unknown and unmapped peaks south of the Romanche, an area into which no Englishman had yet penetrated.

The conquest of this whole range, first of those peaks in the more central groups such as the Pennines and the range of Mont Blanc, later of those in the groups to the east and the west, went

9 A Group on the Mer de Glace above Chamonix

through a number of phases, the most important of which was the Golden Age which started with the conquest of the Wetterhorn by Alfred Wills in 1854 and ended with the ascent of the Matterhorn by Whymper and his party in 1865, by which time the Meije, in the Dauphiné, was the only great peak in the Alps which had not been climbed. The Silver Age followed, lasting until the turn of the century and being marked by the development of guideless climbing, by the climbing of old mountains by new routes, by climbing in ranges beyond the Alps, by the development of climbing in Britain, and by the increase of mountaineering among women.

Wills' ascent of the Wetterhorn in 1854 is generally taken as marking the start of "sporting" climbing. It was not the first ascent of the mountain, whose early history is still being unravelled by scholars, but it was the one which became best known both through the story which Wills told to his fellow-climbers when he returned to London, and the description of the ascent which he later gave in the *Wanderings*. The Wetterhorn's position in the forefront of the view from Grindelwald, a village already being visited by hundreds of travellers each year, helped to make this ascent by a travelling Englishman on his honeymoon the one event which in the eyes of many people marked the creation of a new sport.

During the following few years, men went out to the Alps from Britain in increasing numbers. In 1855 the highest peak of Monte Rosa was reached without guides by the Rev. Charles Hudson, the finest amateur of his day, and a party of young Cambridge men. The Dom in the Eastern Pennines fell in 1858 to the Rev. Ll. Davies, and the Eiger to Charles Carrington. Among the other great peaks of the Alps, the Rimpfischhorn, the Aletschhorn, and the Bietschhorn fell to British climbers in the following year and so, in 1860, did the Grand Paradis, the Grande Casse, and the Alphubel.

By the turn of the sixties, the stream of activity was in full flood, and by 1865 more than a score of the major Alpine summits which had defied the native Swiss were beaten into submission by the carefully swung axes of British climbers and their guides.

The Dauphiné, that queer, lovely country south of the main Alpine chain, hung out longest after the Matterhorn tragedy of 1865, and it was not until 1877 that the first chapter of Alpine conquest was definitively closed with the ascent of the Meije by a remarkable Frenchman, Boileau de Castelnau.

Throughout the whole of the period which began with the exploration of the 1840's and has continued until the present day, there has been what a Government department might call a progression of amenities throughout the Alps.

Four things, above all, differentiated the Alps of that distant era from the Alps of today. First, the men who stepped up on to them stepped into the unknown. Secondly, there was a complete absence of Alpine huts. Thirdly, there was the lack of what modern climbers would consider even the most elementary weight-saving equipment. Fourthly, there was the ameliorating cheapness of guides and porters.

The first of these factors was by far the most important.

> There seemed [said Whymper of the Matterhorn in 1860] to be a cordon drawn around it, up to which one might go, but no farther. Within that invisible line gins and effreets were supposed to exist—the Wandering Jew and the spirits of the damned. The superstitious natives in the surrounding valleys (many of whom firmly believed it to be not only the highest mountain in the Alps, but in the world) spoke of a ruined city on its summit wherein the spirits dwelt; and if you laughed, they gravely shook their heads; told you to look yourself to see the castles and the walls, and warned one against rash approach, lest the infuriated demons from their impregnable heights might hurl down vengeance for one's derision.

Although this was, of course, merely the opinion of one man upon the reaction of his guides to one mountain, it was a typical reaction even in 1860; it was even more typical a decade earlier. "The cordon up to which one might go" was a real thing psychologically for many of the Victorian mountaineers, and a very real and far more substantial one for the Swiss guides who travelled with them and gave them the benefit of their long experience with the mountains.

The lack of huts would probably be even more disconcerting for the mass of Alpine travellers. The *gite* beneath the stars, or at best beneath an overhanging rock, was the rule for the pioneers rather than the exception. There were, of course, innumerable porters on demand to carry blankets; there were guides at relatively cheap rates who could reconnoitre the most suitable spots for the overnight bivouac; there still remained the open air, the uncertainty of the morrow, the awaited step into what was at best the little known. Of modern weight-saving equipment such as wind-proof clothing, condensed foods, and nylon rope, the pioneers had none. Their ladders, which they occasionally carried in order to cross the more difficult spots on a glacier, were of heavy wood; their clothes were very largely those of the British countryside, heavily manufactured articles only slightly adapted to the needs of the Alps. Their boots were, in many cases, merely stout walking shoes locally hobbed.

It is doubtful if the fourth factor, the cheapness of man-power, the fact that porters were available to carry the straw or the shawls, to pack the fuel for the fire and to carry the relative luxuries, ever made up against contemporary standards for the fact that it was customary to sleep in the open or in the roughest of bivouacs. It is doubtful if all the porters made up for the clothes that were unsuitably designed for high altitudes or for the lack of boots, breeches, ropes, or ice-axes specifically designed for the job. The climbers of the 1850's and the 1860's were in fact of a toughness that is rather astonishing. It has been said that no one other than the Victorians could have withstood the cold and harshness of certain Royal homes; it is equally true that many modern climbers would hardly be willing to follow in the steps of the mountain pioneers with only the equipment that was used by them.

Mountaineering, in those early days, required little equipment and an equally small amount of expert knowledge. One result of this happy set of circumstances was that during the early years of the Golden Age the Alps abounded in young University men whose means allowed them to spend a pleasant holiday in the centres lying in a great half-moon around the Alps, and to sally out, as and when they wished, into voyages of exploration. It also allowed, perhaps rather surprisingly, the male members of a large number of young married couples who spent their honeymoons on the Continent, to combine fidelity with an occasional rumbustious Alpine excursion. Wills, Hudson, Kennedy, and Frederick Morshead are only some of those climbers who insisted on spending their honeymoons in the Alps. Leslie Stephen's *Regrets of a Mountaineer* are well known.

The cost of climbing, in its early days, was not large. The one exception was the ascent of Mont Blanc which held its price of about £30 per person until Hudson and his party broke the guides' monopoly with their guideless ascent from St. Gervais in 1855. Yet in 1862 the young John Stogdon, who hired a good guide, who travelled throughout the Oberland for ten days and who must have been abroad for almost double that time, records that he had only £19 for his holiday. As late as 1880 Frederick Gardiner, that steady and conscientious climber from Liverpool whose record of ascents almost equals in number that of Coolidge—a man, moreover, who by no means stinted himself in the benefits of life—talked of £50 for his general expenses, and of £25 for guides, for a six-week season.

It was only rarely that one came upon such a man as the innkeeper below a previously uncrossed pass who replied, when objections to his bill were raised, that "he had carefully reflected upon the matter, and had come to the conclusion that no one would ever come in any case, and that, therefore, he had better charge when he had the opportunity".

The relative cheapness with which one could go climbing, the relative ease of access of the Alps, and the lack of specialised knowledge which it was thought necessary to have, meant that a whole host of people were drawn up into the mountains who in spite of their genuine interest finally remained only on the fringe of mountaineering.

Following Ruskin, there were the artists such as George Barnard, who in 1841 carried out a long Alpine tour with his brother-in-law, Michael Faraday, and their respective wives, and who later became drawing-master at Rugby. Barnard, as his books on drawing prove, had a genuine feeling for mountains, and he was one of the first men to get high among them so that he might draw them accurately. Yet his interest was not that of the mountaineer. He speaks of "the awful solitude of the Alps", and admits: "Although I have for many years found my greatest pleasure in studying amongst the Alps, I have only climbed sufficiently high to obtain the views I wished to paint, finding that if time and strength were spent in climbing there was little left for careful drawing." It is a measure of the Victorians that he should add: "It is not surprising that, after a long day's walk of thirty or forty miles, the sketch then made should be hasty, or thrust aside at the welcome sound of the dinner-bell."

There were many such as Barnard, more courageous than Ruskin, inheriting the knowledge of the previous ten years, helping to prepare the way for the men to whom the business of climbing was the main thing that mattered.

There were many such as Oscar Browning, the queer Eton master, sacked through a dispute in which he expressed his own point of view at the cost of all things, a man with a perceptive yet dilettante approach to the mountains.

> My chief motive for Alpine travel was health [he admitted] and as to its beneficial results in that respect there can be no doubt. I could not have got through my work at Eton without it.

His attitude was almost that of the Philistine, and probably, too, typical of that outer penumbra of young men who were attracted only superficially to the mountains. "I have always maintained that the three most exciting emotions I have ever experienced have been fox-hunting, mountaineering, and standing for Parliament", he wrote later, "and I do not know which is the most exciting of the three." Browning, in many ways representative of those who were tested by mountaineering in early life and found wanting, revealed himself when he admitted that: "One became tired of living upon a knapsack, and never being absolutely clean, of seldom sleeping in a decent room or enjoying wholesome food, and when September arrived I began to long for the fleshpots of civilisation."

Some men were of sterner stuff. The lack of wholesome food, the lack of the decent room that so often meant the fleas of the persistent Alpine joke, the frugality, the hardship and the occasional danger—all these were the inescapable necessities for a handful of young men, many of them University students, who during the 1850's travelled through the Alps and employed Swiss guides to take them up a whole host of hitherto unclimbed summits. Their climbing was carried out in a hearty, not to say boisterous, manner. Substantial food and drink formed part of the adventure; there was a casualness about the danger, and good living was mixed with surprise that the mountains could, and did, suddenly play tricks on those who were climbing them.

Few passages of Alpine literature summon up these qualities of the early days better than one in a paper which Thomas Hinchliff contributed to *Peaks, Passes and Glaciers*, that anthology of mountain experiences which was to precede the *Alpine Journal*.

> The provision knapsacks were emptied and used as seats [says Hinchliff]; bottles of red wine were stuck upright in the snow; a goodly leg of cold mutton on its sheet of paper formed the centre, garnished with hard eggs and bread and cheese, round which we ranged ourselves in a circle. High festival was held under the deep blue heavens, and now and then, as we looked up at the wonderful wall of rocks which we had descended, we congratulated ourselves on the victory. M. Seiler's oranges supplied the rare luxury of a dessert, and we were just in the full enjoyment of the delicacy when a booming sound, like the discharge of a gun far away over our heads, made us all at once glance upwards to the top of the Trifthorn. Close to the craggy summit hung a cloud of dust, like dirty smoke, and in a few seconds another and larger one burst forth several hundred feet lower. A glance through the telescope showed that a fall of rocks had commenced, and the fragments were leaping down from ledge to ledge in a series of cascades. The uproar became tremendous; thousands of fragments making every variety of noise according to their size, and producing the effect of a fire of musketry and artillery combined, thundered downwards from so great a height that we waited anxiously for some considerable time to see them reach the snowfield below. As nearly as we could estimate the distance, we were 500 yards from the base of the rocks, so we

thought that, come what might, we were in a tolerably secure position. At last we saw many of the blocks plunge into the snow after taking their last fearful leap; presently much larger fragments followed; the noise grew fiercer and fiercer, and huge blocks began to fall so near to us that we jumped to our feet, preparing to dodge them to the best of our ability. "Look out", cried someone, and we opened out right and left at the approach of a monster, evidently weighing many hundredweights, which was coming right at us like a huge shell fired from a mortar. It fell with a heavy thud not more than 20 feet from us, scattering lumps of snow into the circle.

The incident was experienced, one feels, more with interest than with fear; almost with a belief that such things were inevitable when one ventured into the unknown regions of the Alps.

Hinchliff himself, a barrister whose wealth obviated the need for practising, was typical of the early mountain-travellers on whose explorations the Alpine Club—which held many of its early meetings in his chambers—was founded. He was leisurely, outspoken, and independent: he described himself as the poacher of Mont Blanc, for when he made the climb in 1857 he refused to employ the stipulated minimum of eight guides but successfully made the ascent with half the number. He made few spectacular expeditions, although he climbed both the Altels and Monte Rosa twice, made the first ascent of Mont Blanc by the Ancien Passage since the accident to Dr. Hamel's party in 1820, climbed the Finsteraarhorn, and made a large number of minor excursions. He wandered rather than climbed, but he knew—as Ruskin did not—that beneath the light shed by danger and difficulty the climber might see a world very different from that presented to the less adventurous traveller. The real lover of the mountains, he stressed more than once, "finds in his most difficult excursions, not merely an exciting and adventurous sport but the enjoyment of a new sensation—that of being brought into immediate contact with the brilliant wonders of an unknown world".

Hinchliff first visited the Alps in 1854, at the age of twenty-nine, and only eight years later was disabled in a shooting accident which forced him to divert his activities to less strenuous travel. His influence on the development of climbing was due to his "clubbability", the extent of his interest in all things pertaining to mountains, and the publication, in 1856, of his *Summer Months among the Alps,* a book which together with Wills' *Wanderings among the High Alps,* had a decisive effect.

Alfred Wills, son of a J.P., a financially well-set-up fellow, coming to maturity in the expansive years that preceded the Great Exhibition, was in many ways the laboratory specimen of the early Victorian mountaineer. Barrister, Judge in the Queen's Bench Division—he was the man who tried Oscar Wilde—he is of importance in the Victorian mountain hierarchy for three separate reasons.

He was, first, the prototype of those gentlemen whose ordinary mountain wanderings developed into genuine mountain-climbing. His experience came slowly, and he travelled in the Alps for many years without attempting a major peak. Throughout the whole of his life, difficult mountaineering was merely one of the attractions which he found in the Alps. He took his wife to Switzerland for her honeymoon so that she might, as he said, be shown some of the glories of the glaciers. And it was on his honeymoon that he accomplished, almost accidentally it might seem, his famous ascent of the Wetterhorn.

Wills was, secondly, one of the first of the Alpine pioneers to forge the relationship between guides and their employers that was one of the great features of the Golden Age. He dedicated his *Wanderings* to Balmat, "my guide and friend, my tried and faithful companion in many difficulties and some dangers". And in much of his subsequent writing he dropped the word "guide" and referred to Balmat solely as friend. It was only to Balmat that he would entrust his wife on her mountain-wanderings while he, Wills, made some more ambitious excursion. And it was Balmat who helped in the purchase of the plot of land in the Valley of Sixt where Wills built The Eagle's Nest for the wife who was to die before she crossed the threshold. In all this there is ample evidence that Wills, more than most men, had such confidence in Balmat that he helped to create, in the guides, what Lord Schuster has called "a new race of men".

Thirdly, there was the ascent of the Wetterhorn, and the story of that ascent which Wills gave to the world in the *Wanderings*. The ascent was by no means the first of the mountain; nor of that particular peak of the Wetterhorn; nor even of that particular peak from that particular side. It was, however, the first that was to gain any measure of notice outside the small select group of Alpine devotees. That fact, combined with the spectacular and engaging form of the peak, its proximity to Grindelwald, a village from which the mountain was so readily visible, and the exciting duel played out on the mountain between Wills' party and the two local Grindelwald men who finally made the ascent with him, combined to give a certain importance to the ascent which has turned the date of 1854 into that when "sporting" mountaineering is popularly supposed to have begun.

Wills first visited the Alps at the age of eighteen, while still a student at London University, and during it made merely a single visit to the Jardin. Four years later he went back, crossing a number of minor passes, visiting Zermatt and making, from Interlaken, the first recorded ascent of the Schynige Platte.

In 1852 he went out again, spending nine weeks abroad and making a number of pleasant if unspectacular excursions—the crossings of the Tschingel, Monte Moro, Allalin, and Theodule Passes—and visiting Chamonix for the first time. From the mountaineering point of view it was hardly an important season, but one record that Wills has left casts an interesting light on the costs of the day.

> We were out nine weeks [he later wrote], one week of which was passed in Paris, where the expenditure was, of course, much above average. We spent no small sum in guides and carriages, and although economical stinted ourselves in nothing. The trip cost us less than £40 each, everything included.

It was in 1853 that Wills first appears to have embarked with full vigour on an Alpine career. Early in the year Forbes had invited Balmat to visit him at his home at Clifton, and Wills had been invited to meet the couple in London.

I was [says Wills] greatly struck by the absence of false modesty or bashful timidity from his bearing. And, although he might sometimes be guilty of a conventional solecism, in all graver respects he was sure to speak and act like a gentleman.

The details of Wills' meeting with Balmat in the Alps later in the same year form an interesting commentary on the Trade Union atmosphere which then permeated the guides' community at Chamonix, ham-stringing initiative wherever possible, putting a premium on mediocrity, and doing much to channel every line of endeavour up the one "routine" peak of Mont Blanc. The crux of the system was the rota, on which every registered guide—the only ones allowed legally to work—was duly entered. Many of the men, possibly the majority of them, were mere glacier guides, "worthy to carry a lady's shawl on the glacier", yet incapable of new or major expeditions. Many were illiterate; only a few, of which Balmat was one, had fought their way up until they had more than a passable knowledge of practical science and were invaluable to such scientists as Forbes. Yet under the rota system such men as Balmat were lumped together on the list with the near-incompetents. And, a subject continually contested by the Alpine Club, any climber coming to Chamonix was forced to take the man at the head of the rota, however useless he might be for the project in hand.

It was in vain that you expostulated—you had an old friend on the list—you did not like the look of the guide thus fortuitously presented—another had been recommended to you—this had nothing to do with the matter [protested Wills]. Superior skill, energy and competency brought no advantage to the good guide; impertinence and incapacity were no disqualification to the bad guide.

So pernicious was the system that one English mountaineer left a substantial cheque for the sufferers from a disastrous fire at Chamonix—on the condition that it should remain untouched until an English traveller was allowed to choose his own guide and to determine for himself just how many men he should take on any particular expedition.

It was unlikely, however, that the wit of the Victorians would be unable to find some way of evading such scandalous regulations. One such method was discovered by Wills or, quite possibly, recommended to him by Forbes. If a guide were hired beyond the jurisdiction of the Chamonix Commune and brought to Chamonix *by way of a col* (those being the operative words) then the traveller who arrived with him was allowed to keep his companion, whatever might be the latter's place on the rota.

Wills had therefore arranged to meet Balmat at Sallanches and to reach Chamonix by the Col de Voza, a ruse which enabled him to keep the guide for a season which was, as it turned out, cut short by bad weather.

The following year he was back on his honeymoon, made a number of minor ascents, spent a night with his wife on the Mer de Glace so that she might see the beauties of the place, took her up the Torrenthorn, and then decided that before he returned to London he would make the ascent of one major peak.

> I had crossed many a lofty col, and wound my way among many a labyrinth of profound and yawning crevasses [he wrote later]. I had slept on the moraine of a glacier, and on the rugged mountain-side, but I had never yet scaled any of those snowy peaks which rise in tempting grandeur above the crests of cols and the summits of the loftier passes.

His choice fell on the Jungfrau, and Balmat suggested that they should consult a local guide. This was Ulrich Lauener, the "tall, straight, active, knowing-looking fellow, with a cock's feather stuck jauntily in his high-crowned hat", a guide who quickly explained that owing to the lateness of the season the Jungfrau could only be tackled from the far side of the Oberland, an expedition for which Wills had not the time. The Finsteraarhorn and the Schreckhorn were both rejected for similar reasons, and only then did Wills suggest the Wetterhorn.

Lauener suggested, presumably with his tongue in his cheek, that the matter was possible and that the Herr might, in any case, like to make a first ascent. Wills rose to the bait, travelled up the valley to Grindelwald with his wife and, a few days later, set out for the Wetterhorn.

With him there were: Balmat; Auguste Simond, a Chamonix guide whom Balmat knew and who had happened to be in Interlaken—a guide who had once held a fully grown man off the ground at arm's-length and who was soon nicknamed "Samson"; Ulrich Lauener, who was in charge of the party; and Peter Bohren, another Grindelwald man who had been to the plateau from which the three Wetterhorn peaks all spring, at least three times that season.

On the mountain, after a rough bivouac, the party found itself being outflanked by two mysterious figures, one of whom carried a fir-tree on his shoulder, a tree comparable to the "flag" carried by Lauener which was in fact a great sheet of iron attached to a 12-ft. mast. After a great shouting-match carried out across the snows, it was learned that the two men were local chamois-hunters, Christian Almer and his brother-in-law Ulrich Kaufmann, both of whom were to win fame as guides. Hearing of the attempt by Wills' party, they had decided to climb the peak for the honour of their native valley, had brought the fir-tree to place on the summit beside the iron "flag", and had climbed the lower crags during the night. Eventually, both parties joined forces and reached the summit together.

As they went higher on the mountain, the mood of the party altered. "One must never shout on the great peaks," Balmat warned Wills, "one never knows what will happen." The local Grindelwald men might be less impressed, but both for the Chamoniard and for Wills there was a new wonder as they trod through the summit ridge and saw "a few yards of glittering ice at our feet, and then, nothing between us and the green slopes of Grindelwald, nine thousand feet beneath".

Wills' reactions at that moment, when he broke through not a physical but a mental barrier raised by the unknown, provide a clue to the whole inner driving force of Victorian mountaineering.

> We felt [he wrote later] as in the more immediate presence of Him who had reared this tremendous pinnacle, and beneath the "majestical roof" of whose deep blue Heaven we stood, poised, as it seemed, half-way between the earth and the sky.

He was there, he knew, on sufferance. He had a great humility. Mountaineering, he might have said had he lived a hundred years later, had added to both his intellectual and his emotional stature.

At first glance, there was a whole multiplicity of contradictory reasons for the climbing carried out by the young men of Wills' time. Some climbed because they desired to explore, and the Alps formed the most convenient field for their exploration. Some climbed "for the exercise". Some climbed for a sight of the majestic scenery which could not be viewed, as Ruskin had imagined, from the bottom of the mountains. Yet the common denominator, which could be seen more clearly as the century progressed, lay outside the realm of material experience. It lay, rather, in the realm of the inner spirit, enclosed in a dissatisfaction with the great material progress of the age, a dissatisfaction which it was rarely possible and even more rarely expedient to express.

This is shown in the composition of one group of men, four or five of whom were associated in a whole list of important climbing expeditions during the 1850's. There were the three Smyth brothers, Charles Ainslie, Charles Hudson, and E. S. Kennedy, and it is significant that three of them—two of the Smyths, and Hudson—were clergymen, while Kennedy, who wrote *Thoughts on Being* at the age of thirty-three and who was renowned for his persistent question, "Is it right?", seriously contemplated taking Holy Orders. They were all "serious" young men; they all gave considerable thought to the problems which the growing knowledge of science was creating; and they all appear to have found in their climbing some solace from the troubles of the world that was something more important than mere escapism.

Hudson was the finest mountaineer, not only of the whole group but of the whole generation, the man who was "almost as great as a guide", and who was even more largely responsible for the conquest of the Matterhorn than was Whymper. He spent the winter of 1852–1853 in Switzerland—he was then twenty-four—and reconnoitred a new route up Mont Blanc, returned to England where he was ordained, and then went to the Crimea where he served as Chaplain with the Forces and, after the fall of Sebastopol, went for an adventurous trip across Armenia and approached Mount Ararat. Returning to the Alps in 1855 he made, with the Smyths and John Birkbeck, the first ascent of the highest point of Monte Rosa, an expedition in which the guides followed the amateurs. A week later, he made the first guideless ascent of Mont Blanc, an event which the guides did everything in their power to prevent. He continued to climb almost every year until his marriage in 1862—contriving, indeed, to visit Zermatt during his honeymoon—and returned to the Alps in 1865 when he introduced the young Douglas Hadow to the Alps and, a few days later, was killed with him on the Matterhorn after having made the first ascent of the mountain with Lord Francis Douglas and Michael Croz (both of whom also perished), Whymper, and the two Taugwalders.

Hudson, being more competent than any of his contemporaries, found it necessary to remove, from between the mountain and himself, as it were, the third party which consisted of the guide. The acclaim which greeted the ascent by Kennedy and himself of Mont Blanc was only partially due to the fact that such guideless climbing lifted a large financial weight from the shoulders of youthful Alpinists. It gave also a sense of satisfaction totally different from that gained from any climb in which guides took part.

In some cases the guides trod carefully in the rear, but even then their inborn experience of the weather, of just what risks could be taken with any particular set of circumstances, was always available in reserve. With guideless climbing, the amateurs were forced to stand four-square by their own judgements. Once they had reached the ability of a Hudson it was only thus that they could fairly face the facts of mountaineering life.

It was not until later that guideless climbing fell into disrepute, largely due to the antics of the Rev. Girdlestone who appears to have been protected from disaster only by exceptional luck and who published in 1870 the story of his travels in *The High Alps without Guides*, a book that created considerable controversy and which, in the opinion of many, did the cause of climbing a serious disservice.

The Matterhorn itself was first climbed without guides in

1876 by Cust, Cawood, and Colgrove, three sturdy exponents of private enterprise, while the Meije, the last of the great Alpine peaks to be conquered, was climbed without guides by the Pilkingtons and Frederick Gardiner in 1879, only two years after it had first been climbed with professionals. The Pilkingtons, Lancashire business men, were typical of the second generation of Alpine pioneers, men of strong character who sought in guideless climbing and in the development of British mountaineering a relaxation from the multiple duties of a life crammed with service, industry, and hard work, the coin in which the Victorians bought their leisure.

The apogee of the guideless climbing movement came early for the Victorians, in this period of the young Hudson. "One is much inclined to think that, at one period, these Hudsons, these Smyths, these Ramsays, these Parkers, these Youngs, these Buxtons, and others were within measurable distance of diverting the stream of English mountaineering from the course it eventually took and of forming a great school of guideless English climbers", wrote Captain Farrar, that great Alpine expert. As history finally ordained it was only the experience of the Second World War, combined with the financial stringency imposed by post-war restrictions, that was to begin the formation of such a school.

Hudson wrote but little. Together with Kennedy, he described his ascent of Mont Blanc without guides in *Where There's a Will There's a Way*, and to a second edition he added his account of the Monte Rosa expedition. He contributed an occasional paper to *Peaks, Passes and Glaciers*, and notes to the *Alpine Journal*. Yet nowhere did he even begin to explain those inner reasons for his obsession with mountaineering of which there are occasional hints in his scanty writings.

This is more to be regretted because the development of mountaineering during the later 1850's owed so much to the books which its exponents were beginning to make available to an ever-growing public. There had, of course, been many mountain books before the mid-fifties, but they had been written for a restricted and almost family public. From the first ascent of Mont

Blanc, a whole succession of little pamphlets had appeared upon the scene, something like four for every five ascents of the mountain which had been made. They were detailed, honest, and intimate little journals, telling exactly what had happened to the conquerors, recording the names and weaknesses of the guides, explaining what was, or was not, seen of the view from the summit, and recording in understandable detail the great reception accorded in Chamonix to those who had paid some £30 apiece for the ascent. They were frequently subsidised by their authors.

The little books were invariably slim, expensive, well bound, well printed, illustrated by sketches or water-colours of those artists who had known Mont Blanc at least at distant range, and were sometimes privately produced for circulation almost exclusively among the friends of those who had made the ascents recorded. They make fascinating reading, but their contemporary influence was negligible.

The mountain books of the mid-fifties were different. Even Forbes' *Travels through the Alps of Savoy*, a book largely for scientists, had contained much of interest to the general reader. Wills' *Wanderings*, Hinchliff's *Summer Months among the Alps*, Hudson's account of his Mont Blanc ascent, and, to a lesser extent, *The Spirit of Travel*, a handy little book by that mountain-connoisseur, Charles Packe, who travelled through both the Pyrenees and the Lakes with his dogs—all these books were intended for the less clearly defined reader. Their circulation, even so, was influential rather than large; their reviews were in the right places and were discussed by the right people. They gave, to mountaineering in the later 1850's, a position it would hardly otherwise have occupied. They formed the bridgehead from which the intellectual assault could be launched.

That the bridgehead was built up at all was largely the result of a lucky chance which brought Hudson to Longmans, the publishers. William Longman, later to become Vice-President and then President of the Alpine Club, was at the time of Hudson's ascent of Mont Blanc one of the heads of the firm. He not only published Hudson's book but later in 1856 made his first Alpine tour. He was forty-three at the time, and his age combined with his family responsibilities to prevent him from ever seriously tackling the business of mountaineering; yet he was fascinated by the Alps and by all that he saw in them, and in the following year gladly published Hinchliff's *Summer Months among the Alps*. He was invited to become a member of the Alpine Club, and was one of the moving spirits in the publication of *Peaks, Passes and Glaciers*, as well as the publisher of a whole host of Alpine books that included Wills' sequel to the *Wanderings*, Tyndall's *Mountaineering in 1861*, and Gilbert and Churchill's *Dolomite Mountains*, the first account by Englishmen of the remarkable area—a mountain area through which, like many other Englishmen, they had first travelled on their respective honeymoons.

Longman, like most successful publishers, had most of his fingers on the unpredictable pulse of the public. He sensed, rightly as it turned out, that the isolated adventures which had followed Forbes' explorations were already being transformed into the permanent background and tradition of a pastime with a steadily increasing body of devotees.

The next move was obvious.

Chapter Three

THE ALPINE CLUB

Love of mountains, like the love of nature is something new, perhaps sophisticated. I cannot help that. In me it is too deeply implanted to be rooted out.

HENRY W. NEVISON

THE growing interest in the new and frequently criticised occupation of climbing mountains for pleasure must, in the Victorian Age, have had one inevitable result. It was obvious that a group of like-minded men would form themselves into a club whose members would meet at pre-arranged intervals to discuss the technical aspects of their interest, to exchange information and, if the record of human nature stands for anything, to spur themselves on to further efforts.

The result was the Alpine Club—*the* Alpine Club and not the London Alpine Club or the British Alpine Club. There was no need for any geographical location for this, the first organisation of its kind; in any case, the calm clear assumption of superiority fitted well into the spirit of the age. It had, after all, been *the* Great Exhibition, unqualified by any adjective. The Alpine Club therefore assumed, at its inception, a certain dictatorial rightness—to which it had, it must be admitted, almost every possible claim. It began in an age when it could, through the unique experience of its members, speak, as it has spoken ever since, with something of the authority which belonged to the Delphic Oracle. There was, at times, more than a hint of God about it. To the men who formed the club nearly a century ago the communal views which they expressed must have seemed, in an Alpine context, to be rather like the voice of God Himself.

The earliest suggestion that an Alpine Club should be formed came from William Mathews, the first of a long line of Alpinists from the great Worcestershire family whose members swam into success on the crest of the Victorian wave, in a letter to the Rev. Fenton John Anthony Hort.

Hort, a typical Victorian ecclesiastic of great mental power whose equally vigorous climbing potentialities were limited by ill-health and overwork, had been a friend of Mathews at Cambridge and had made a number of climbs with him. He was known even in his early days for sound common sense and administrative ability, and it was natural that Mathews should write to him. For Hort was then a Fellow of Trinity, a college to which a high percentage of the early climbers had belonged, and it was likely that he, above all other men, would be able to judge the possibilities.

> I want you to consider [said Mathews in his letter of February 1, 1857] whether it would not be possible to establish an Alpine Club, the members of which might dine together once a year, say in London, and give each other what information they could. Each member, at the close of any Alpine tour in Switzerland or elsewhere, should be required to furnish, to the President, a short account of all the undescribed excursions he had made, with a view to the publication of an annual or bi-annual volume. We should thus get a good deal of useful information in a form available to the members.

Hort agreed to the idea but feared that the dining might have precedence over the information to be exchanged; care, he warned, should be taken that the dinner bills were kept within reasonable dimensions.

That summer Mathews visited the Alps with his cousin, Benjamin St. John Attwood-Mathews, and together with Kennedy they discussed the formation of an Alpine Club. Finally, on the thirteenth of August they made the first English ascent of the Finsteraarhorn, together with the Rev. J. F. Hardy, and a Mr. Ellis. The success of the expedition further encouraged the idea of a club and its formation was definitely decided upon. That autumn William Mathews, his son, Mr. St. John Mathews, two of his nephews, W. and C. E. Mathews, together with Kennedy, dined at William Mathews' home, The Leasowes, on the outskirts of Birmingham—the house where the young Edward Whymper was later to tell Forbes the story of the Matterhorn accident. The name of the house is still seen on even the quarter-inch Ordnance Survey maps, retained, perhaps, by a cartographer who knew not only that the poet Shenstone had lived there but that it was the birthplace of the Alpine Club.

At The Leasowes dinner, Mathews and his friends drew up lists of men likely to join the Club; Kennedy, on his return to London, either saw personally or wrote to all those on the various lists. A few men showed little interest. The rest met at Ashley's Hotel, Covent Garden, on December 22 and the Club was formally established.

Kennedy had previously circulated a note listing the objects and proposed rules of the Club, and it is obvious from some of the reactions to this that the original idea of a dining club which would meet once a year had already expanded considerably.

> The chief point which raises doubt is the expense [wrote Hort, who was unable to be present at the December 22 meeting]. On what do you propose to expend guinea subscriptions and guinea entrance fees? Surely there is nothing to be gained by having "rooms", "curator", and that style of thing? William Mathews wrote to me about such a club for *one* dinner nearly a year ago: and I then told him I thought it would be an excellent thing, provided the dinner bills were kept within reasonable dimensions. When he was here a few weeks ago, he quite concurred; he was going to write to you on the subject, but I have heard no more from him. Is it not rather much to ask a guinea a year, besides *two* dinners and (for all except Londoners) two double journeys to town? Granting that it is desirable to make the club select, we cannot see that a money standard is a desirable one. It may be well to have a few books and maps, though most of us would be likely to possess the best maps of districts which we meant to visit; but their annual cost ought to be something very small. Circulars would also cost something. But these are the only necessary expenses we can think of (except in connexion with dinners, which will, as you propose, be divided among the diners); and they might annually be divided among the whole Club without a large fixed subscription. What idea lurks under "geographical explorers" and "other guests of celebrity"?

Surely we do not want speeches from Dr. Livingstone or Sir Roderick Murchison? The introduction of such elements seems likely to impair the genuineness of the whole affair.

In spite of such rather querulous complaints Hort became an original member and remained a member until his death in 1892.

The one real controversy at the formation of the Club consisted of the argument that soon developed around Rule XII. This laid it down that all candidates should have ascended to the top of a mountain 13,000 ft. in height—a curious qualification since mountaineers had soon learned that height itself was rarely a measure of difficulty. The rule was finally amended so that a candidate's general mountaineering ability and experience, rather than any one isolated effort, became the criterion. Furthermore, it was made clear that, in certain cases, men who were not active mountaineers might be eligible for membership. The objects of the Club were, after all, defined as "the promotion of good fellowship among mountaineers, of mountain climbing and mountain exploration throughout the world, and of better knowledge of the mountains through literature, science, and art".

Mr. John Ball, the Irish politician, scientist and traveller, who had been Under-Secretary for the Colonies in Lord Palmerston's Administration of 1855, was elected the first President of the Club early in 1858. His choice was not due to the prestige afforded by his name for at that time he was one of the most experienced of all Alpine travellers; although he had made few spectacular ascents, he had been travelling throughout the Alps for nearly twenty years at the time of his election, had crossed the main chain forty-eight times by thirty-two different passes, and had traversed nearly 100 of the lateral passes.

The Club was now fully launched on the world, but not for another year did it acquire permanent quarters. Its members continued, instead, to meet in Hinchliff's chambers in Lincoln's Inn and to hold their dinners in various hotels and private rooms. The reason is explained by William Longman who some twenty years later wrote a short history of the club and embarked on a history of mountaineering whose completion was cut short by his death.

It was at first assumed that the Club would take the character rather of a social gathering of a few mountaineers than of a really important society, at the meetings of which papers were to be read, and contributions made to the geographical and topographical knowledge of mountain regions, and it certainly never entered into the mind of any of its founders to conceive that it would be the parent of fruitful children, each more prolific than itself.

Within a year, membership had risen to more than eighty. By 1861 it had reached 158, and claims to membership were being based on "a list of literary contributions or mountain exploits". The Club was expanding, not only as Hort had apparently feared, into a wining and dining club, but into Longman's "really important society". The less ascetic side of life was by no means neglected, however, and Ellis Hardman, the "Victorian Pepys" as he has been called, has left a typical picture of an annual summer dinner.

Last night I dined at the Castle, Richmond, with the Alpine Club [he wrote]. We found a jolly party round William Longman, the publisher, who is Vice-President of the club, Anthony Trollope sitting next to him. Longman is a glorious fellow, full of jokes and story, and beaming with good humour. Anthony Trollope is also a good fellow, modelled on Silenus, with a large black beard. There was a call for Trollope, and Silenus made a funny speech, assuring the Club that he was most desirous of becoming a member, but the qualification was the difficulty, and both time and flesh were against him. He added that not very long since, in the city of Washington, a member of the U.S. Government asked him if it were true that a club of Englishmen existed who held their meetings on the summits of the Alps. "In my anxiety", he said, "to support the credit of my country, I have transgressed the strict limits of veracity, but I told him what he heard was quite true" (Great cheers).

Through all the vicissitudes of the Club—and it was rent, at fairly regular intervals, by fierce arguments on policy, procedure, and almost everything else, which all the contestants appear thoroughly to have enjoyed—a certain civilised "clubbability" remained uppermost. Small cliques or groups were formed from me to time, though rarely for a more harmful purpose than oncentration on some specific Alpine problem or the gratification of some mutual interest. This was true, for instance, of the lub within a club whose headed note-paper bore an embossed est which included a black waiter on the left, a green guide on e right, a black-and-blue shield in between and, below, the ords "Curre per alpes".

The history of the device on the paper is as follows [explained A. W. Moore, one of the most enterprising and daring climbers of the 1860's, and one of the first to climb in the Caucasus]. A small number of A.C.'s have for years past dined together before the meetings, and the device is their private property, now superseded for postcards! The man in black symbolises a waiter, he in green a guide—the sole idea of the community being dining and climbing. The bloody hand grasps a—carving knife. The falling figure is prophetic of the fate which will not improbably befall us, while the Chamois grins with serene happiness from the elevated and exalted position which the faller vainly strove to reach! Altogether a cheerful allegory!

The facts, dates, and figures of the early members of the Alpine lub have been tabulated in a great labour of love, the three-olume *Alpine Club Register* which was compiled over long years careful research by the late A. L. Mumm. From this Sir rnold Lunn has abstracted figures showing that of the first 1 members of the Club—those who joined it between 1857 and 63—fifty-seven were practising barristers, twenty-three were licitors, and thirty-four were clergymen, with landed gentry and ons coming next with nineteen and fifteen respectively. Many of e Club's early members, however, had little more than a passing terest in mountaineering. Matthew Arnold—"everyone should e the Alps once, to know what they are"—was a member. So as Wilfrid Scawen Blunt. Sir Richard Burton was elected though he never completed his membership), his qualification ing "General travel; mountain ranges in all parts of the world". was Thomas Atkinson, from Cawthorne, Yorkshire, that odd aveller of humble origin, a bricklayer's labourer and quarryman ho rose to fame through his architectural ability, travelled across much of Central Asia for the Tsar, and on his return to Britai succeeded in maintaining a position of some public importanc despite the fact that he had two wives living in Britain simul taneously, a feat by no means common even today.

Once those members who had little genuine interest in moun taineering are removed from the total, the preponderance c lawyers, business men, and clergy is even more marked. Most c these were men of considerable learning and scanty leisure. I is significant that for almost all of them travel among the hig mountains was not only a pleasant relaxation but something th appeared to influence much of their lives. There were two mai reasons for this, the first physical and obvious, explainable mo easily by the example of the hardest workers among the busine men and the lawyers; the second more undefined, more difficu of definition, more explicable by the examples of the clergyme and of the scientists.

Many of the Victorians climbed because they found in th mountains the greatest escape from, the greatest contrast to, the normal, densely packed life. At first, as was natural, they wer to the Alps. Later, as climbing techniques improved, as the majc and then the minor peaks of the Alps were climbed, a few of ther looked farther afield for their relaxation. Charles Packe in th Pyrenees, Douglas Freshfield in the Caucasus, and Cecil Slingsb in Norway, all brought the principles of sound mountaincraf developed in the Alps almost entirely by British climbers, t lands which knew little of such matters.

Most cosmopolitan of them all was Freshfield, who made thre journeys to the Caucasus, led an expedition to the Himalaya— where he was seen on occasion in grey cut-away tail-coat an trousers—and who also climbed in South Africa, the Ruwenzor the Canadian Rockies, and the Japanese Alps. Yet howev attractive such ventures might be, lack of time and money pr hibited them for most mountaineers, to whom they appeared isolated and rather exotic departures from the main sport c Alpine climbing.

The one exception to this was formed by the explorations i Norway of Cecil Slingsby, that great Yorkshireman, Elizabetha

11 John Tyndall (*bearded*) outside the Bel Alp with his Wife, 1876

12 The Rev. Hereford George's Party on the Lower Grindelwald Glacier, 1865

13 Lawrence and Charles Pilkington and (*centre*) Frederick Gardiner, in the late 187(

of both frame and outlook, with a name still not only known but honoured in the most unexpected of small Norwegian hamlets.

Slingsby spent five seasons in Norway before he visited the Alps. Later he played an important part in the development of climbing in Britain and when, during the 1880's and 1890's, he carried out his major Alpine campaigns they consisted largely of guideless climbs whose main attractions lay on rock rather than on ice or snow. His traditions, therefore, did not spring so directly from those of the Alpine pioneers as did most of his contemporaries. With mountaineering he linked not science but art; in the mountains he saw not a laboratory but a field for new human experiences which would make every day brighter and better.

To understand why men of his calibre devoted themselves to a sport still under criticism, it is necessary only to consider the record of C. E. Mathews, a benign and much-loved Birmingham man who was an early prototype of the Alpine Club member.

Mumm's summary that for nearly fifty years Mathews made himself felt in countless ways in the public and social life of Birmingham is an under-statement. With Joseph Chamberlain, one of his greatest friends, Mathews was a founder of the National Education League. He was chairman of innumerable committees, president of innumerable societies, a Birmingham Town Councillor, a governor of schools, a leader in local politics, a Justice of the Peace, and an active and opinionated member of a whole galaxy of bodies. He managed to pack all this activity into seventy-one crowded years, to become also, as well as one of the most accomplished mountaineers of his day, an expert of importance on subjects as varied as the Waterloo Campaign, the Birmingham Water Supply, and the detailed history of Mont Blanc.

The mountains provided the clue to this extraordinary energy. Mathews was the text-book example of the man who went climbing to escape—not from any unpleasant facts of life but from the crowded events which his own high standards of duty pushed relentlessly on to his shoulders.

At the bivouacs or in the mountain hotels of the Alps, at the cottage which he later acquired at Machynlleth, in North Wales, Charles Edward Mathews could slough off the responsibilities of Birmingham. Here, he knew, was a relaxation, a safety-valve such as no other sport could possibly provide. Here, surrounded only by amiable companions who like himself wished for a time to turn their backs—at least until the end of the month—on the progress which they had helped to create; surrounded, also, by that new race of men which he had helped to raise from the raw material of the guides; here Mathews and men of similar thought were able to forget the pulsing, scrambling, gainfully employed life of England's expanding industrial empire.

Mathews played an important part in creating the guides as an honourable and respected group of men. For hundreds of years local peasants had been available for leading travellers across the easy snow passes of the Alps. Some of them had helped Hannibal, and their ancestors' ancestors had done much the same job for the men of the Middle Ages who had succeeded in keeping open the great trans-Alpine trade routes. Yet the whole virtue of these men was that they could lead others across mountains rather than up them; they would look, instinctively, for the nick in a skyline rather than for the ridge that led to a summit. Many were good and brave men; many more merited Whymper's description of "pointers out of paths, and large consumers of meat and drink, but little more".

It needed mountaineers such as Wills and Mathews, as the Rev. Hereford George and Leslie Stephen, to raise up a certain number of Alpine peasants, to breath fire into them and to stir into them a knowledge which was eventually to make them the first members of a great profession. In an unexpected way, the Alpine pioneers mixed as perfect equals with these peasants whom they hired. There was something more to it than the remark of one guide to his employer on a mountain that: "You are master in the valley; I am master here." Reading back through the record, catching what one can from the memories that remain, one can really believe that in this way at least some of the Victorians did practise the theory that all men are born equal. "They were just like brothers", said the daughter of one famous amateur and the guide with whom he climbed regularly for more than a quarter of a century.

"To say that I owe him a debt impossible to pay is not to say much," Mathews wrote of Melchior Anderegg, the guide with whom he spent most of his climbing life, and whom he personally guided round the Snowdon Horseshoe on one memorable occasion when Melchior was staying with him in his cottage in North Wales.

> He first taught me how to climb. For more than 20 seasons he has led me—in success and failure—in sunshine and in storm. He has rejoiced with me in happy times; he has nursed me when suffering from accident with a charming devotion. Year after year I have met him with keener pleasure. Year after year I have parted from him with a deeper regret.

Mathews' introduction to the Alps was a hearty one during the season of 1856 when with his brother, William Mathews, he ascended the Dent du Midi, was turned back by weather on Mont Blanc, and during the course of three weeks' successful climbing crossed a number of passes and climbed a number of peaks, including Monte Rosa.

The following year he returned to the Alps, met Melchior Anderegg, and embarked on that long Alpine career that took him to the mountains almost every year until the turn of the century when, at the age of sixty-five, he was reluctantly compelled to give up mountaineering. He had had forty seasons, climbed both the Matterhorn and the Wetterhorn three times, the Mönch twice, Monte Rosa five times and Mont Blanc no less than twelve.

Mathews, inevitably, went to the Alps for his honeymoon, and during the holiday attempted the Blumlisalphorn, climbed the Altels, was turned back on the south face of the Weisshorn, and ascended the Jungfrau with Horace Walker, the Liverpool merchant who together with Mathews was to play such an important part, nearly a quarter of a century later, in the development of climbing in Britain.

Mathews, the epitome of that comfortable God-fearing group of middle-class Englishmen who believed that the Almighty had deliberately put them into positions of responsibility, was charitable, overworked, but only mildly critical of the appalling conditions in which large numbers of his countrymen lived. Perhaps the most characteristic quality of his climbing, and of all that is known about him, was his "clubbability". In this, as well as in his established background and his physical motives for climbing, he was typical of a considerable segment of Alpine Club members. The ascent of a fine peak was, with Mathews, one part of a day's adventuring in which comradeship with others, the ordered progression of the day from dawn to dusk, the shared enjoyment of fine sights and experiences, the new experience in the regular march of life, all merged to make one civilised and civilising experience.

Few men did more than Mathews to consolidate the foundations of climbing in Britain. With his home on the outskirts of Birmingham it was natural that holidays too short for enjoyment in the Alps should be spent in North Wales, where he climbed Snowdon more than 100 times and Cader Idris more than 100. It was Mathews who did so much to bring fame and fortune to Pen-y-Gwryd, the little inn standing where the road from Capel Curig forks uphill towards the summit of the Llanberis Pass and downhill towards the distant gleam of Llyn Gwynant. Here, in 1870, he founded the "Society of Welsh Rabbits", a small group of friends banded together to explore Snowdonia in winter, and it was Mathews who played an important part in the foundation, in 1898, of the Climbers' Club, of which he was to become first President.

He was an honorary member of both the Yorkshire Ramblers Club and of the Rucksack Club. He was an adviser, a man of experience whose views, all knew, would be completely disinterested as well as fully informed. He was utterly reliable and fair, and in his later days occupied much the same position as that filled half a century later by Geoffrey Winthrop Young.

Mathews represented all those constant qualities of which civilisation is compounded. For the Alpine Club he might well have been a symbol, the "typical climbing man" against whose character and record the critics might beat in vain.

Chapter Four

THE SCIENTISTS

The sea of faith
Was once, too, at the full, and round earth's shore
Lay like the folds of a bright girdle furl'd.
But now I only hear
Its melancholy, long, withdrawing roar.

MATTHEW ARNOLD

MATHEWS was typical of that large body of Alpine Club members who found in the mountains the complete and incomparable break from the Victorian world which they had helped to create. Yet to escape into the mountains was only one incentive for the climbers of the Golden Age; the demands of science formed another.

The early scientists who first solved the basic problems of high mountain-travel had their counterparts a decade or more later in such men as Bonney, Tuckett, Ramsay, John Ball, and Tyndall. Some were to help in the development of mountain-wandering into the craft of mountain-climbing; some were to see the transformation of the craft into the organised sport of the twentieth century.

The scientists of mountaineering's Golden Age can be divided into the amateurs and the professionals. There were those such as Francis Fox Tuckett, a man bristling with note-books and instruments, an indefatigable and earnest amateur whom hard times never limited, a lucky man whose mountain and scientific inclinations happily coincided. And there were the professionals such as Tyndall, the poor boy from County Carlow, whose scientific work took him into the mountains, the boy who later found circumstance taking him to the mountains year after year and himself going to them for love alone. The amateurs had the mountain passion earlier in their lives than the professionals, and moulded their lives to fit their inclinations. The professionals were captured unawares by the mountains, often in middle life; their passion appears to have been deeper and more disturbing because of this fact.

There were, of course, those men such as Bonney, a scientific Mathews, who in all difficult problems returned again and again to the mountains for a solution. With Bonney, as with so many of the Victorian mountaineers, it is his energy and his many-sidedness that astound. At the age of sixty he walked from his hotel to the top of the Piz Languard, an ascent of about 4,800 ft., "without a single pause", as he proudly puts it. Well past the age of seventy he maintained his regular seven miles a day, fair weather or bad, and at the age of eighty was still capable of what his not uncritical Alpine friends called strenuous days on the hills. His range of interests was of the size which might have been expected of that rarity, the geologising parson. To the climber, Bonney is the man of twenty-seven who unsuccessfully tackled the Pelvoux—when even its position was unknown—two years before Whymper visited the Dauphiné. To the geologist he is one of the pioneers. To the ecclesiastics, one of those preachers who remained calm and undismayed by the terrors of Darwin. He was a mountain sketcher of considerable ability, an extensive producer of books and sermons, an architectural artist of almost professional skill, and the writer of more than 200 separate articles, most of them in the full-bodied many-columned fashion of the day.

Thomas George Bonney was only eight or nine when he was first impressed by a great mountain view—that of Snowdon from the garden of the Royal Hotel at Capel Curig, looking to the mountains across the Mymbyr Lakes. It was a view that he never forgot, and its effect remained with him for the rest of his life.

At the age of twenty-three he made his first visit to Switzerland, a rather routine visit with a reading party during which he journeyed across the Mer de Glace but did no serious climbing. He took Holy Orders—his religious service was almost entirely limited to two years as curate at St. John the Evangelist, Westminster and, later in life, two years as Cambridge Preacher at the Chapel Royal, Whitehall—and returned to the Alps two years after his first visit. He crossed a number of passes, became interested in the problems of high climbing, and returned the following year to climb the Altels and Monte Rosa.

It was in 1860 that he turned to the Dauphiné, driven there largely by the zest that is, as he put it, "given to the pleasure derived from the beauties of nature by the knowledge that they have been seldom or never seen by others".

Forbes' notes on Dauphiné, published seven years earlier, comprised all the printed information available. The atlases, comments Bonney, did not recognise the existence of mountains in that part of France, while the most reliable map of the country which had been made was that of Bourcet which had been completed more than a century ago—in days when the presence of dragons in the Alps was first being seriously disputed.

With the spread of mountaineering in the sixties, the inns of the Dauphiné became notorious, and there is little doubt that they were far more ill-kempt than those of the rest of the Alps. Bonney's description of what faced him and his party—consisting of the ubiquitous William Mathews and John Clarke Hawkshaw, a Manchester civil engineer who remained a member of the Alpine Club until his death in 1921 though he had not climbed since the 1860 season—was not, however, so very untrue of the rest of the Alps in the days of the pioneers.

> On the great high road from Grenoble to Briançon there is fair accommodation at one or two places [he said]. Off this, everything is of the poorest kind; fresh meat can only be obtained at rare intervals, the bread and wine are equally sour, the auberges filthy, and the beds entomological vivaria. It is hardly possible to conceive the squalid misery in which the people live; their dark dismal huts swarming with flies, fleas, and other vermin; the broom, the mop and the scrubbing brush are unknown luxuries; the bones and refuse of a meal are flung upon the floor to be gnawed by dogs, and are left there to form an osseous brecia. The people in many parts are stunted, cowardly and feeble, and appear to be stupid and almost *cretins*. Too often there, as in other parts of the Alps, "every prospect pleases and only man is vile".

When it came to the "entomological vivaria", Bonney's

scientific knowledge was useful. There was the time, he recalls, when he and a companion had the choice of two beds in a very small inn. One of the beds looked relatively trim; the other was filthy. They tossed a coin, Bonney won—and took the filthy bed. In the morning his companion found that while he had been wracked with insects, Bonney had been untroubled.

"Yes," he quietly explained, "I chose the iron bedstead; they don't breed them."

On the mountains one was apt to have similarly unpleasant surprises. In 1860, when Bonney and his companions set out to climb Mont Pelvoux, then still vaguely thought to be the highest peak in the Dauphiné, they had been told of a rough hut on the mountain in which they could bivouac. Finally the guide pointed it out:

> a huge mass of rock that had in former times fallen down from the cliffs above, and had rested so as to form a shelter under one of its sides. This had been still further enclosed with a rough wall of loose stones, and thus a sort of kennel was made, about nine or ten feet by five or six, and about four feet high at the entrance, whence it sloped gradually down to about two feet at the other end.

Finally, the party was turned back by bad weather, as it was two days later on Monte Viso, and Bonney moved south to Turin with Hawkshaw, finally going to Zermatt over the Theodule and spending the rest of his holiday in the Zermatt area.

The remoteness of the Dauphiné fascinated Bonney as it was later to fascinate others, and to it he returned again and again in the following years until he finally became, with Tuckett and Coolidge, one of the greatest British experts on the group. His travels took him, however, to almost every part of the Alps. First a Lecturer in Geology at St. John's, then, for a quarter of a century, a Professor of Geology at University College, London, he became increasingly aware of the vast number of scientific problems which could be solved in the laboratory of the Alps far more easily and conveniently than elsewhere.

The extent of his wanderings is shown by the fact that in thirty-five seasons he made about 110 ascents, six of them above 10,000 ft., and crossed more than 170 passes.

Less of a professional scientist than Bonney, more of a mountaineer, yet the man even more responsible than Coolidge for the encyclopaedic approach to the Alps, was John Ball, the Alpine Club's first President. The creator of *Peaks, Passes and Glaciers* and, through that, of the *Alpine Journal*, as well as of the *Alpine Guide*; Ball was not only politician and amateur scientist but, more than these things, a gentleman of leisure, treading the familiar path from University to Bar and then devoting himself to those useful pursuits in which men of less time and less money could not indulge. He was, almost alone among the early British mountaineers, a prominent Catholic.

Like Bonney, Ball was first influenced by mountains at the early age of nine when he first saw the Alps from the Col de la Faucille. Perhaps nothing, he said later, had had so great an influence on his entire life.

He was, as might have been expected from a Catholic, more interested than Bonney, or most contemporary scientists, in the spiritual experiences which the mountains offered. While in many ways typical of the Victorian amateur scientist, begirt with notebooks, he yet had a genuine love of pioneering work which went far beyond his note-taking needs. It was the interest of making a difficult passage, rather than any scientific urgency, which compelled him in 1845 to press on with his crossing of the Schwartzthor, on which he finally led his incompetent guide across the pass. It was the same reason, twelve years later, which impelled him to press on to the summit of the Pelmo, one of the first great Dolomite peaks to be climbed.

It was possibly in 1845, the year in which he was called to the Irish Bar, that Ball first appreciated how well mountain-wandering might be combined with his scientific observations. He spent some time at Zermatt, chiefly engaged in the double task of exploring the remarkable vegetation of the Valley of St. Nicholas, and of observing the movement of the two nearest glaciers. He climbed the Riffelhorn, made a number of glacier excursions, then returned to Zermatt and made the first passage of the Schwartzthor.

Thereafter he travelled in the Alps almost every year until his death in 1889, covering their whole breadth by his excursions, making new ascents wherever these fitted into his plan for fresh botanical or geological observations, but travelling rather than climbing, gaining knowledge of a whole area rather than "working out" any one valley, a process which might, had he adopted it, have given him a list of first ascents as fine as that of any of his contemporaries. By 1863, when the first volume of his *Alpine Guide* appeared, he had crossed the main Alpine chain forty-eight times by thirty-two different passes and had in addition traversed nearly 100 lateral passes—a record which at that time was unique.

Ball has left a description of how he travelled and what he took with him, a description which cannot be very dissimilar from that of most scientists of the time who carried their amateur researches into the Alps.

> To my knapsack [he observed] is strapped a stout piece of rope about thirty feet long, with a Scotch plaid and umbrella; the last, though often scoffed at, is an article that hot sunshine, even more than rain, has taught me to appreciate. A couple of thermometers, a pocket klinometer, and a Kater's compass with prismatic eye-piece, may be carried in suitable pockets, along with a note-book and a sketch-book, having a fold for writing-paper, etc., a good opera-glass, which I find more readily available than a telescope; strong knife, measuring tape, a veil, and spectacles, leather cup, spare cord, and matches. A flask with strong cold tea, to be diluted with water or snow, a tin box for plants, a geological hammer of a form available for occasional use as an ice-axe, with a strap to keep all tight, and prevent anything from swinging loosely in awkward places, complete the accoutrement.

The fact that Ball's journeys were planned with eyes on scientific rather than mountaineering records is well illustrated by the list. It was not, however, so strange that it was Ball who was asked to fill the Presidency of the Alpine Club in 1858, an office left vacant when the Committee had been elected. His position in the world, his administrative ability, and his retirement from politics early in 1858 which gave him the time to devote to a pleasant hobby-horse, all combined to make him an ideal man for the post, especially as the Club at that time represented a pastime whose aims and ideals were, at the best, imperfectly understood. There was also not only Ball's Alpine record but the feeling that his particular brand of knowledge would enrich the Club, arising as it did from his practice in the orderly, logical presentation of facts. The Club had not long to wait.

In November, Ball wrote to William Longman.

> Among the crowd of tourists who leave England every year, a good many visit places of interest in the Alps and elsewhere, that are nearly or quite unknown to the reading public. A fair proportion of them are capable of writing an intelligible and even interesting account of what they have done and seen, but with limited materials it is neither reasonable nor desirable that each should write *a book*. What would you say to bringing out an *annual volume*, made up of contributions of travellers? If carefully selected, I should say that such a volume would be generally interesting, and secure of a large sale. Unlike the books of most travellers, the writers would have no occasion to *stuff* their articles with additional matter taken out of libraries; there would be room for small contributions to science, especially Natural History, but in that department especially I would advise you (if you should adopt the idea and undertake the *editing*) to use much stricter restraint than most book-writing travellers exercise over themselves. People of limited information are apt to record facts which are either already well known and familiar to men of science, or else wanting in the needful precision and accuracy. A little previous communication with the writers might sometimes convert a loose statement into a useful fact.

Thus, with an aim that was more scientific than Alpine, there was born the germ that developed into *Peaks, Passes and Glaciers, A Series of Excursions by Members of the Alpine Club*. The first volume in the series, in which there were recorded many of the now near-legendary exploits of the pioneers, was published by Longmans early in 1859, under Ball's editorship. By the end of the year it had gone through four editions totalling 2,500 copies, and a fifth edition was issued in the following year. Two more volumes, edited by E. S. Kennedy, and illustrated by woodcuts prepared by Whymper, appeared in 1862, and their success confirmed the earlier impression that a "regular market" now existed for chronicles of Alpine exploration. The next year there followed the *Alpine Journal*, that "record of mountain adventure and scientific observation" that has remained the weightiest if not the final word on all matters of Alpine history, topography, and etiquette.

Great as were the benefits which the publication of such material accorded the climbers of the mid-sixties, they were as nothing compared with the lasting effect of Ball's *Alpine Guide*. As early as 1861, Ball had pointed out to a meeting of the Club that there existed no guide-book for mountaineers that dealt with the whole chain of the Alps. The result was his commission to produce such a guide, and the eventual publication of his great trilogy, *Guide to the Western Alps* (1863), *Guide to the Central Alps* (1864) and *Guide to the Eastern Alps* (1868). Scores of helpers were co-opted into the work, their information being sifted, checked, and edited by Ball, who was in a vast number of cases able to tally the facts and figures against his own experience. "Ball", together with *Peaks, Passes*, and the volumes of the *Alpine Journal* itself, became one of the craft's Sacred Works, and one which, unaltered, was regularly consulted until its rewriting and reissue by Coolidge at the end of the century.

Second only to Ball in the extent of his Alpine wanderings, in his encyclopaedic and scientific approach to the mountains, and in the earnest vigour with which he carried out his campaigns, was Francis Fox Tuckett, the Bristol Quaker and business man who between 1856 and 1874 climbed 165 peaks, 84 of them important summits, and crossed some 376 passes. No less than 57 new expeditions were included in these figures, an indication that Tuckett's scientific interest was well tempered with the desire for pioneer work.

Like Mathews, he packed an astonishing amount of work into every day. Discussing one of his mountain campaigns with Coolidge—for nearly a month they once wrote one another a letter every other day—he mentions in passing that he is writing thirty or forty letters a day, running his complicated and extensive business, and is also busy with an executorship and sundry trusteeships.

After a visit to Switzerland as a child Tuckett returned in 1854, at the age of twenty, for a long rambling tour. Two years later he met Forbes and was imbued by him with the need for contributing to the body of scientific knowledge, whatever else he did in the Alps. "Make mountaineering not merely a recreation, but a scientific occupation" is reputed to have been the gist of Forbes' exhortation.

Tuckett followed the advice, and the majority of his journeys were made with all the equipment necessary for detailed observation and recording. He bristled with instruments, and his deep pockets were filled with a series of elaborately organised notebooks and pencils ready both for making the pleasing panoramas which graced his records and for their detailed annotation.

> He was a sight to see [said Hort in 1861], being hung from head to foot with "notions" in the strictest sense of the word, several of them being inventions of his own. Besides such commonplace things as a great axe-head and a huge rope and thermometers, he had two barometers, a sypsieometer, and a wonderful apparatus, pot within pot, for boiling water at great heights, first for scientific and then for culinary purposes.

It is easy to ask why all this conglomeration of scientific impedimenta was needed. The answer is that there were still men, even in the early days of "sporting" mountaineering, who genuinely considered that any failure to record a multitude of facts, figures, and dates, would be a back-sliding in social and moral duty. They may have been right.

Even so, a sense of proportion was needed, and Tuckett's ponderous contributions to *Peaks, Passes and Glaciers* invoked Leslie Stephen's mock-heroic account of an ascent of the Gabelhorn. On this famous climb, the scientists discovered the temperature by the amount of cold on their fingers, for the thermometer was broken, and found it to be 175 degrees below zero; their height was so great that the mercury in the barometer sunk out of sight. "As to ozone," said Stephen, "if there *were* any ozone that afternoon on that arête, ozone must be a greater fool than I take it to be." Professor Tyndall, for whom the Alpine Club rules had been altered so that he might become Vice-President, resigned in protest after Stephen's bantering speech, thinking the barbs meant for him.

There was, in fact, less reason for Stephen to jibe at Tyndall than at Tuckett. Tyndall was taken to the mountains by the practical business of earning his own living and to him men like Tuckett must have been rather ponderous dilettantes, however charming their character might be and however useful might be the vast gathering of information on which they lavished so much of their time, hardiness, and money.

Information Tuckett certainly did gather, ream upon ream of it, both during his own high mountain excursions and on the less strenuous tours which he made in middle life with his sisters. Throughout the 1860's and 1870's he returned, year after year, to the Alps, climbing with most of the mountaineers of the day; getting his one, or more, first ascent per season; planting his thermometers carefully on peaks and passes where they could be consulted, and their readings taken, by later travellers; winning from the King of Italy the Order of St. Maurice and St. Lazarus for his scientific and geographical investigations in the Alps; and only refusing the Presidency of the Alpine Club because he felt that residence in or near London was essential to the job. Slow, rather ponderous one must imagine, with an almost Germanic lack of humour, Tuckett yet ventured in his measured stride on the verge of more narrow escapes than most of his more adventurous contemporaries. There was the famous time beneath the Eiger when his party escaped destruction beneath an avalanche by a matter of feet, an escape described in *A Race for Life*. He was arrested as a spy on the Austrian frontier in 1866, and three years later as a Panslavist agitator; while, right at the end of his last season of hard climbing, in 1875, he finished his final expedition by taking cover on the Roche Melon in a chapel which was almost immediately partially destroyed by lightning.

Tuckett had at least one thing in common both with Forbes, the master who had preceded him, and with Tyndall, his fiery contemporary. All three believed that it was the moral duty of the mountaineer, the man moving up into new kingdoms, to equip himself mentally and physically for carrying out the maximum number of useful scientific observations. Forbes had found a certain pleasure outside these observations. So did Tuckett in a rather shame-faced sort of way. Tyndall took his observations seriously, for they were both his life's-work and his bread-and-butter. Yet without a hint of inconsistency he admitted the glory of climbing for its own unscientific sake. What is more, he explained the fact with a clarity which itself explains the motives of Mathews and his kind and took the argument one step farther.

> I have returned to them every year [Tyndall wrote of the Alps], and found among them refuge and recovery from the work and the worry—which acts with far deadlier corrosion on the brain than real work—of London. Herein consisted the fascination of the Alps for me; they appealed at once to thought and feeling, offering their problems to one and their grandeur to the other, while conferring upon the body the soundness and the purity necessary to the healthful exercise of both.

The belief in this dual function of mountains was almost the only thing that Forbes and Tyndall had in common. Only twelve years separated their births but in social background and religious beliefs, Forbes belonged to the eighteenth century and Tyndall to the nineteenth. Forbes, his whole life conditioned by a wealthy and conservative family background, saw the Alps for the first time on a "Grand Tour" that was almost part of the social round. Tyndall saw them first on the student's walking tour of 1849 of which he later said that "trusting to my legs and stick, repudiating guides, eating bread and milk, and sleeping when possible in the country villages where nobody could detect my accent, I got through amazingly cheap". Even in their religious beliefs, the contrast between Forbes and Tyndall was striking, Forbes feeling the principles of the Church as governing his everyday habits and actions in a way that was near-medieval; Tyndall remaining, in spite of all his efforts, the confirmed agnostic who wished for no stone to be raised above his grave.

In spite of all these differences it was Tyndall who occupied in the mountaineering world of the 1860's the pre-eminent position that Forbes had occupied a decade earlier. Both had a good background of what the Victorians called substantial worth; both could only with danger be accused of rashness or imprudence, and the journalist who wrote the famous leading article in *The Times* after the Matterhorn disaster—"Is it life? Is it duty? Is it common sense? Is it allowable? Is it not wrong?"—must have had some anxious moments wondering if Tyndall would open a broadside against the attack. Much of Tyndall's importance to the Victorian mountaineers and their development lay just in this fact; that he was an unassailable, stabilising body whose scientific theories might be questioned only with care, whose religious doubts might be deplored, but whose interest in the new sport of mountain-climbing was an inexplicable fact that must be accepted as the idiosyncrasy of an intellectual heavyweight whom it would be unwise to cross.

Tyndall's first holiday walking tour in 1849 took him from the quiet German university town of Marburg (where von Papen was later to make his one unavailing denouncement of the Nazis) On September 19 he marched south, arriving at Heidelberg thre days later in the true fifty-mile-a-day fashion that he retained unti late in life. In Heidelberg he decided, as he wrote later, to "se how the mountains appeared under such a sky. In those days i was a pleasure to me to saunter along the roads enjoying such snatches of scenery as were thus attainable. I knew not the distan mountains; the attraction which they afterwards exercised upo me had not yet begun to act."

What is more, it failed to act even when he came within sigh of the Alps, perhaps because of his unfortunate approach, throug Zürich, Zug, and Arth to the Rigi, the notorious Rigi where thirty years later, the immortal Tartarin of Alphonse Daudet wa to be surprised by "that immense hotel, the Rigi-Kulm, glaze like an observatory, massive as a citadel, wherein for a day and night a crowd of sun-worshipping tourists is located". Fo Tyndall it was, rather similarly, merely a cloudy mountain note for its guzzling and its noise.

14 Ulrich Almer saving his Employers on the Ober Gabelhorn, 1880
From a drawing by H. G. Willink

15 With his Guide, Melchi
Anderegg

16 On one of his later visits
to Grindelwald

He continued farther into Switzerland, saw the Rhône Glacier, had an awkward scramble to the Grimsel after he had lost his way, crossed the Little Scheidegg where he saw the avalanches on the Jungfrau, and then turned back for home. "The distant aspect of the Alps appeared to be far more glorious than the nearer view", he commented, in an almost Ruskinian manner that was enough to show that he had not, by then, been intrigued by mountains at first hand.

His conversion was not to start until seven years later when, following his interest in the problems posed by the cleavage of slates, he went to Switzerland in the hope of being able to answer the questions by investigating the glaciers. The journey was made with Professor Huxley, and Tyndall proudly recalls that he received his alpenstock from the hands of Dr. Hooker, in the garden of the Pension Ober, at Interlaken. Thence, he set out on a tour that included visits to the Guggi, the Lower Grindelwald, the Unteraar and the Rhône Glaciers—a tour from which it might well be claimed that there was to spring all his later preoccupation with mountaineering.

Tyndall's interest in the subject appears to have gone through two distinct phases. There was first the era of scientific enquiry that began to change in 1859; and there was an era of the great expeditions which followed 1859, many of them still linked to important scientific enquiries but planned also with the aim of mountain conquest.

It is possible that Tyndall's love of the Alps was born in 1856, during his scientific ramble with Huxley. His description of what he calls the exceedingly grand scene on the Little Scheidegg is revealing.

> The upper air [he said] exhibited a wild commotion which we did not experience; clouds were driven wildly against the flanks of the Eiger, the Jungfrau thundered behind, while in front of us a magnificent rainbow, fixing one of its arms in the valley of Grindelwald and, throwing the other right over the Wetterhorn, clasped the mountain in its embrace. Through the jagged apertures in the clouds, floods of golden light were poured down the sides of the mountain. On the slopes were innumerable chalets, glistening in the

V.M.—6

sunbeams, herds browsing peacefully and shaking their mellow bells; while the blackness of the pine-trees, crowded into woods, or scattered in pleasant clusters over alps and valley, contrasted forcibly with the lively green of the fields.

This was the description not only of the scientist but of the embryo mountain-enthusiast and it was hardly surprising that Tyndall went back the following year, by this time greatly involved in the glacier argument and already at loggerheads with Forbes. He stayed at the Montanvert for six weeks, taking measurements as Forbes had done, crossed the Col du Géant, and ascended Mont Blanc with a boy.

Once he got among the mountains, Tyndall appears to have shown a sense for hill form and scenery almost entirely alien to the rest of his life, inclinations, and aptitudes. Almost as soon, he developed a love of daring mountain adventures, many of which—such as his solitary ascent of Monte Rosa in 1858 with merely a bottle of tea and a ham sandwich as supplies—would have been rashness in the case of any man less competent.

The competence showed itself immediately Tyndall took to serious climbing, and from the later 1850's his record is a peculiar mixture of high ascents which would have been "pure" mountain ascents in the case of any other man but which were, in his case, carried out largely for scientific motives, and of hit-and-thrust exploits which equalled those of any member of the Alpine Club.

In 1858 he climbed the Finsteraarhorn to make observations from its summit while Ramsay made comparable measurements from the Rhône Valley, thousands of feet lower. The following year he made his famous ascent of Mont Blanc with Sir Alfred Wills and August Balmat, during which the latter placed important scientific instruments in the summit-snow and nearly lost his hands by frost-bite in doing so. When Tyndall returned to England at the end of the season he persuaded the Royal Society to vote a grant of money to Balmat in recognition of his services to science. By that time Tyndall had made yet another ascent of the mountain, during which he spent twenty hours on the summit.

All these ascents could have been justified by Tyndall as adjuncts to his scientific enquiries. Like Forbes he was investigating the glaciers. Like other scientists he was concerning himself with the properties of air, of light, of sound, and he could claim that many of his investigations demanded that observations be made on high mountains.

Yet in 1860 Tyndall actually tried to climb the Matterhorn. To realise just what this meant it is necessary to remember how Albert Smith had been assailed for climbing Mont Blanc, a mountain higher than the Matterhorn and therefore, according to the current theory, far more worth while so far as scientists were concerned. If there were no new facts to be found on Mont Blanc there were certainly none—of scientific importance, at least—to be found on the Matterhorn. Yet Tyndall went at it almost bull-headed, discarding much of his scientific shroud and standing up, unashamedly, as one who wished to step beyond that "cordon up to which one might go". What is more, he succeeded in reaching a height of 13,000 ft., a height considerably beyond that which men had yet reached on the mountain. Tyndall, the scientist at the height of his energy and fame—he was just forty at the time—was beginning to enjoy mountaineering for its own sake.

The following year he went to the Alps with one idea in his mind, that of climbing the Weisshorn, then one of the "last problems" of the Alps. He did so successfully, with Johann Joseph Bennen, the enigmatic Valais guide who almost reluctantly accompanied him on the great enterprise. From then onwards Tyndall lived as a mountaineer in his own right, unsupported by scientific necessities. He was already making climbs far more difficult than those tackled by such men as Forbes or, for that matter, by any man in mere search of scientific data. He was moved by the spirit of combat and risk that the mountains offered him; from the position of a man who carefully exploited the mountains for their scientific value, he had marched in a few strides to the other end of the calendar. There is a touch of the "death-or-glory" boys about some of his exploits.

I followed him while the stones flew thick and fast between us [he says, of Bennen on the Old Weisthor in 1862]. Once an ugly lump made right at me; I might, perhaps, have dodged it but Bennen saw it coming, turned, caught it on the handle of his axe as a cricketer catches a ball, and thus deflected it from me.

He was, we may surmise from his record, a man who was titillated by danger, and across all his worthy, learned, and essentially dull scientific record there is drawn the shadow of another man, the man whom duty prevented him from being on more than isolated occasions. He would, says an eye-witness, delight picnic parties by hanging from his heels from the highest trees to be found. In the Alps, where the little Marjelensee bordered the great Aletsch Glacier, he would jump on to the nearest miniature icebergs and balance on them until they finally gave him the inevitable cold bath. On his stray visits to Cornwall he would sometimes be found clambering with unexpected interest up some of those northern cliffs which have since exercised the ingenuity of both the Climbers' Club and the Commandos.

He was, parallel with his stern, calculating scientific exterior, a genuine mountain adventurer, seeing in small rocks as well as in great mountains the challenge of physical matter. At the height of his scientific fame he was the only man other than Whymper who believed that the Matterhorn would one day be climbed. The full story of his efforts to justify the belief can be pieced together only from his *Hours of Exercise in the Alps* and from Whymper's *Scrambles*. The two men clashed, as might have been expected. Had either Tyndall or Whymper had less similar mountain ambitions, they might have joined forces in the early 1860's—as Whymper was later to join forces with Hudson—and have climbed the mountain before that fatal day in 1865 that influenced all Alpine history.

As it was, Tyndall stood on the touch-lines of the Matterhorn story, a position in which his actions are revealing of his impetuous, tenacious, yet analytic character. For it was Tyndall who after the accident of 1865 seriously suggested the fantastic scheme of having himself lowered down the Matterhorn precipices by some 2,000 ft. of rope in an effort to find Lord Francis Douglas' undiscovered body. And it was Tyndall who in 1868 made the first traverse and the seventh ascent of the Matterhorn, climbing the mountain from Breuil, in Italy, and descending to Zermatt in Switzerland.

Thus, he made few high Alpine ascents. Overwork, illness, and marriage, all contributed. Yet so soon as he had the funds he built, on the Lusgen Alp near the Bel Alp, the ugly Villa Lusgen from which he might look across the Rhône Valley to what he considered was the most beautiful view in the Alps. He spent much of his time at Hindhead, where his house, the first to mar that lovely spot, still looks down the Happy Valley to the distant gap in the South Downs where the nick of the highroad crosses the last barrier to Portsmouth and the open sea. He loved high places. He loved the beauty he found there, however disturbing and unscientific might be the emotions which it aroused.

In all Tyndall's relations with mountains, other than those which are astringently scientific, there is some feeling that he gained from them an awareness of life and death that he would otherwise have missed. He thought the danger worth while. They were, for him it seemed, an educator whose value was almost as great as that of science. They enabled him to enjoy life more, to put more into it and to take more out. Had he approved the word, Tyndall might almost have claimed that the mountains were a religion. For many Victorian scientists it appears that they were a substitute for something which their own religion had failed to give them.

Chapter Five

THE CLERGY

It is something to have wept as we have wept,
It is something to have done as we have done;
It is something to have watched, when all men slept,
And seen the stars which never see the sun;
It is something to have smelt the mystic rose,
Although it break and leave the thorny rods;
It is something to have hungered once as those
Must hunger who have ate the bread of gods.

G. K. CHESTERTON

THE age in which the specialised craftsmen of the Alpine Club worked out the details of their sport was something more than an age of religious belief. It was an age in which all religious belief was being challenged with a wealth of apparent evidence that had not been seen for some considerable time. There were questionings, and they involved the whole basis of religious truth on which many Victorian mountaineers had founded their lives. They were the result not only of the onward stumble of science in general, but of the growing knowledge that illuminated one particular aspect of science.

This aspect was archaeology, or the story of man's past. It was just possible to consider the theories of the earth's creation eons before the date laid down in the Bible and yet still keep a hold on belief. The problem became altogether more difficult when the discoveries in the Somme Valley, made by Boucher de Perthes and confirmed by a reputable if unofficial British commission of enquiry in 1859, placed the beginnings of man's history at least some hundreds of millenia back.

Dr. Joan Evans, in *Time and Chance*, has well described the impact which these discoveries had on the mind of Victorian man.

> The establishment of the existence of palaeolithic man [she says] did more than add chapters to human history. It added vast stretches of time to those ages which even the most anthropocentric philosopher must consider; it destroyed the conventional chronology of Church and University; it brought a new proportion into man's view of the cosmos, that was only comparable with the change of proportion brought about by the Renaissance discovery of a new world.

It is not to be wondered at that this attack on belief, unintentional though it might be, should have had an equally disturbing effect both on those who made it and on those at whose beliefs it was directed. It was, after all, the Eternity of the scientists as well as of the clergymen which was suddenly being lifted away from heir future.

It would be presumptuous to claim that many of the Victorian clergymen who went mountaineering did so, even indirectly, to reassure themselves about an after-life; or that the scientists did so to prove to themselves that their revelations had not really altered life. The thinkers of the period did not really climb because they witnessed in the mountains some newly seen yet constant physical phenomena in a changing world. The scientists among them were only too well aware of the fallacy disguised by he phrase "the everlasting hills". The clergy found that their guides, those well-tried mountain friends, still believed in many mystic goings-on that had little to do with Christianity.

Yet the blunt truth is that many deeply religious men did find, during their mountain excursions, some satisfying reinforcement to their beliefs. The first and most obvious reason for this was that many mountaineers, then as now, found their sense of God heightened, illuminated, and justified by their physical experiences in the mountains. Wills on the Wetterhorn, feeling "as in the more immediate presence of Him who had reared this tremendous pinnacle", was typical. So was Charles Hudson, who after John Birkbeck's escape on the Col de Miage—he was only nineteen when he slid some 1,800 ft.—put down the escape to what he called a "long chain of providential arrangements due . . . surely to Him who guides and protects us day by day". Whymper himself, troubled with doubts throughout his lifetime, and even at his most emotional hardly a religious man, reveals in the carefully self-edited *Scrambles* at least some shadow of that feeling which crossed his mind when after the Matterhorn accident two great crosses hung in the sky before the eyes of the horrified survivors. The references to God and His near Presence, regular as they are in the Alpine literature of the day, were not written in by the pioneers as a matter of conventional form. They were felt and experienced, and those feelings and experiences were doubly deep because of the doubts which had, for a while, flitted across the mind.

The problems created by the impinging of science on religious thought lie at the nub of the matter. Without their impetus, mountaineering would not have shot forward with such jet-propelled speed during the second half of the nineteenth century. It was natural, therefore, that the clergy should play an important part in its development. Many were not clergy as one would use the word today. University regulations being what they were, it was normal—in many cases essential—for those wishing to prosper in an academic life to take Holy Orders. Some, such as Hereford George, the first editor of the *Alpine Journal*, who devoted his talents largely to military history and mountain-climbing, never held even a curacy. Many, such as Coolidge, found that neither the taking of Holy Orders nor the minor work of a small parish necessarily involved any thundering or militant work of protestations. A few, like Leslie Stephen, resigned Holy Orders as their opinion of the world developed and as they stepped more clearly out into it; others, such as George, were ordained only when their feet were about to feel their way cautiously up the ladder of success.

Yet even when such men are taken into account, it seems true that the clergy illuminate better than any other single group, just what it was that drove men of the period up into the hills. For the clergy, more obviously than most, did not climb to demonstrate their physical courage or because they were not so good at organised games. Many of them did, of course, revel in the toughening and heroic business of climbing difficult mountains diluting it where necessary by the use of suitable guides. But they might have taken equal risks in any of a dozen other dangerous pursuits. They chose mountaineering for the simple reason that it could, and did, provide something that no other pastime did offer. What that almost indefinable quality really was, can best be inferred from the fact that the serious thinkers appreciated it most. For it was a moral quality. It was a satisfaction of the mind rather than of the body. It was a window through which man saw his own justification. It was something which in some inexplicable way restored his dignity and confidence and belief in life. It was something that reassured the clergy among whom so many enthusiastic mountaineers of the period were counted.

Of the suggested members of the Alpine Club who replied favourably to Kennedy's circular which he issued after the "Leasowes" meeting, more than a quarter were clergymen. The Rev. Hort was among them, of course, and so was the future Canon Lightfoot. So was Hardy, Llewellyn Davies, and a number of other clerics whose interest in the Club's activities eventually waned. The first editor of the *Alpine Journal* was George—who was not, however, ordained until after the end of his editorship; the second was Leslie Stephen who relinquished Holy Orders three years after the end of his editorship. The fourth was the Rev. W. A. B. Coolidge—who took Holy Orders while in office.

Hudson, killed on the Matterhorn, was the greatest amateur of his age; Julius Elliott, who in Britain discovered the "ordinary" way up the Pillar Rock and who in Switzerland was the first to follow Whymper's fateful footsteps from Zermatt to the summit of the Matterhorn; Girdlestone, who achieved either fame or notoriety according to one's point of view for his advocacy of guideless climbing; all these were typical of the clergymen who made climbing their one major recreation. It is difficult to discover any aspect of Victorian climbing in which some cleric does not play an important part.

Hudson and the two Smyths had been among the first of the young men in Holy Orders who during the 1850's had helped to create the sport of mountaineering. Yet however great their mountain ability, they were religious flyweights and it was left to

Hort and Lightfoot, both of them among the leading Biblical scholars of the day, to demonstrate the fact that profound religious study mixed well with high Alpine travel.

Hort was the more important of the two in both the academic and the mountaineering sense. He made his first, five-week, tour in the Alps in 1854 at the age of twenty-six, and after only this slight experience returned two years later with most ambitious plans.

> Lightfoot and I [he wrote to the Rev. John Ellerton, one of his oldest friends] have agreed to rendezvous at Luzern July 19th, spend a week in training among the peaks of Uri, etc., ending at the Grimsel, and a fortnight in the snow regions of the Bernese Oberland (the ascent of the Jungfrau and Finsteraarhorn being dreamed of); and then make all haste to St. Gervais at the foot of Mt. Blanc, where we expect to find Hawkins and perhaps Ames or Watson, and thence ascend Mt. Blanc himself (this is a dead secret) by the new route, thereby avoiding the extortions of Chamonix. Lightfoot has made not up his mind how much farther he will accompany us before diverging to Germany, but at all events Hawkins and myself talk of moving eastward, crossing and recrossing the main chain till we reach Zermatt, and then spend some two or three weeks in that region, going up Mt. Rosa and as many other of the highest points (mostly unexplored hitherto) as we can manage, and then return home. I hope we shall find it an expedition to be remembered.

As it turned out, he made the eighth ascent of the Jungfrau and was turned back by weather three times on the St. Gervais route up Mont Blanc which had then been ascended only by Hudson and Kennedy's party the previous year. It was on this visit to the Alps that Hort first tried his hand at mountain photography, carrying a bulky full-plate camera on many of his climbs but failing to achieve results through waiting too long to develop his plates. Many of the early climbers had done their imperfect best to take Alpine photographs. Ruskin claims the credit for what he calls "the first sun-portrait ever taken of the Matterhorn and as far as I know of any Swiss mountain whatever", in 1849. The two Smyths carried about a photographic tent for use on their climbs in the mid-fifties, and G. Joad, who accompanied Hudson and Kennedy for part of their guideless ascent of Mont Blanc in 1855, took a number of photographs, one of which was used as the basis for the frontispiece of *Where There's a Will There's a Way*. And there was the unnamed English colonel whom Mrs. Cole met in the Val Anzasca in 1858, complete with wife, developing tent, and mule for carrying the photographic equipment. Bisson, the Frenchman, made three photographic journeys to the summit of Mont Blanc in 1861, 1862, and 1863, spending five days at the Grands Mulets on his second trip. Yet it was not until Hereford Brooke George made his family tour of the Oberland in 1865, taking with him Ernest Edwardes, a portrait photographer of some standing, that good results above the snowline were achieved by any British mountaineer.

George, more than most of the climbers, "looked the part". With red beard and great height, he was massive and confident both of mind and of body, with a record both on the mountains and in the sphere of Alpine organisation quite equal to the reputation he later acquired as an historian.

He first visited Switzerland at the age of twenty-two and was taken on a minor glacier expedition by Leslie Stephen. He returned the following year, crossed the Monchjoch and climbed Mont Blanc. And he then, having joined the Alpine Club, threw himself with tremendous fervour into the conquest of the Alps' unclimbed peaks and uncrossed passes. The following year he became the editor of the newly founded *Alpine Journal*. He served on a special committee which was set up by the Alpine Club to lay down standards for ropes, axes, and alpenstocks, and he devoted what leisure he had not only to the major problems of Alpine travel but also to the most minor details of equipment. In 1865 he planned and led the ambitious tour through the Oberland made by three ladies and six men, and organised largely with an eye on the photographic possibilities. And, in between the minor excursions made for the benefit of the photographer and of the ladies, he took part in a number of major climbs, including the first ascent of the Jungfrau from the Wengern Alp and the first ascent of the Gross-Nesthorn. Soon afterwards, in the 1870's, he founded the Oxford Alpine Club.

Mountains and mountaineering had captured George's interest and imagination. And, with a fullness that was alien to most of his fellows, George explained carefully just why this was so. The attraction was, he infers, a complex one, half-Jingoist, half-ethereal.

> The climbing spirit [he wrote], like the love of all kindred pursuits, is essentially a form of that restless energy, that love of action for its own sake, of exploring the earth and subduing it, which has made England the great coloniser of the world, and has led individual Englishmen to penetrate the wildest recesses of every Continent.

Yet this was not the only explanation from the young man who was to take Holy Orders two years later.

> The deeper we penetrate into the *arcana* of nature, so as to discern "the law within the law", the more clearly do we perceive that above and beyond all law rises the supreme will of the Almighty lawgiver [he wrote]. Familiarity with the wonders of the Alps is among the best means of originating and deepening such impressions; for their gigantic size and awful phenomena tend to produce an effect not merely on our intellectual perceptions, but also upon the moral feelings.

George, who was about to enter the Church, had, in fact, discovered in the Alps some revelation curiously similar to that found by Stephen who after taking Holy Orders changed his views, ceased to regard himself as a clergyman, and profoundly disturbed many of his friends by his *An Agnostic's Apology*. The mountains, to Stephen:

> represent the indomitable force of nature to which we are forced to adapt ourselves; they speak to man of his littleness and his ephemeral existence; they rouse us from the placid content in which we may be lapped when contemplating the fat fields which we have conquered and the rivers which we have forced to run according to our notions of convenience. And, therefore, they should suggest not sheer misanthropy, as they did to Byron, or an outburst of revolutionary passions, as they did to his teacher Rousseau, but that sense of awe-struck humility which befits such petty creatures as ourselves.

Both George and Stephen had been educated, in the Alps, into

17, 18 On the Mer de Glace in the late 1870's

19 Sir Edward Davidson and his Guides

their own particular brand of humility; they both felt rather like Frederic Harrison's man who needed "sometimes to know nothing and to feel nothing, but that he is a marvellous atom in a marvellous world".

Stephen stands at the heart of the attraction which mountaineering had for the religiously inclined of the mid-Victorian years, just as that attraction lies at the root of its meteoric expansion between 1850 and 1880. A clergyman turned agnostic, Stephen was yet a deeply religious man throughout his whole life. Disturbed as he was by Darwin in a way that Hort never was ("In spite of difficulties, I am inclined to think it unanswerable", wrote Hort, who kept his belief. "In any case, it is a treat to read such a book"), Stephen appears to have created, from his experiences in the mountains, a new belief for the one he had rejected.

He was ordained in 1855, at the age of twenty-three, and the same year made his first visit to the Alps, a rambling-cum-scrambling holiday in Bavaria. Two years later he spent a month in the Mont Blanc area, and ascended the Col du Géant.

It was not until the following year that the mountains began to influence him, that he met Kennedy, Hardy, and Hinchliff at Zürich, and embarked on his meteoric Alpine career. By this time he had been subjected to two influences. He had come under the spell of the Alps themselves, "woven in a great degree by the eloquence of *Modern Painters*"; and he had, as he also admitted, been infected with the Alpine fever by reading Wills' *Wanderings*. From the start of his climbing career he was therefore deeply influenced by two diametrically opposed theories of Alpine appreciation. The result was of considerable significance to the Alpine world, for it made Stephen unique in at least one respect. He could sup in full measure off the most glorious sights that the mountains could offer, and could explain their beauties to others; yet he could also gain equal joy from setting out on expeditions that were invariably difficult, frequently dangerous and, judged by the standards of the Ruskinians, completely useless.

The 1858 campaign was a six-week tour during which Stephen first met Melchior Anderegg, his guide and lifelong friend, and during which he made a number of high ascents, including that of Monte Rosa. The great years commenced in 1859, and for eight seasons Stephen strode up and across the Alps, taking part in a score of first ascents any one of which would have placed him among the most accomplished mountaineers of the day. The first ascent of the Schreckhorn and of Monte Della Disgrazia, the first complete ascent of Mont Blanc from St. Gervais, the first passage of the Jungfraujoch and of the Viescherjoch—these are only a few of the great courses he accomplished in an almost casual manner during the early 1860's.

He was a vigorous, forty-mile-a-day man who covered the country "like compasses over a small-scale map", and who was always proud to have walked the fifty miles from Cambridge to London in twelve hours to attend an Alpine Club dinner. He was the dominating personality in the Alpine Dining Club, whose crest was described by Moore. He was occupied like most of his contemporaries, in a score of different jobs from electioneering to writing, from organising University clubs to pamphleteering; and he was, throughout the whole of his early Alpine career, cogitating on his religious commitments. The doubts had begun in 1862 when he had first refused to take part in Chapel services. Finally, in 1875, he relinquished Holy Orders and began writing the long series of essays later collected as *An Agnostic's Apology*.

Yet Stephen's retreat from Christianity was unlike that of many others. "In truth," he later wrote, "I did not feel that the solid ground was giving way beneath my feet, but rather that I was being relieved of a cumbrous burden." More curiously, his personal actions continued almost exactly along those broad lines of conduct that are followed by most Christians. During the years that he first spent in the mountains he ceased to believe, he felt, in any form of God. Reading today what Stephen wrote three-quarters of a century ago, it is difficult not to believe that what happened was the transmutation of his beliefs into something different, something non-Christian, but something that hardly warrants the word agnosticism.

There followed, after his change of heart and his marriage, both of which took place in the late sixties, another eight years during which his activities in the mountains were limited by the fears of his wife. He made the first ascent of the Cima di Ball, and of Mont Mallet—"that child of my old age" as he called it—and the first passage of the Col des Hirondelles; yet by far the greater part of his holidays were taken up with excursions of minor importance; and, after the death of his wife it was to the newly developing sport of winter mountaineering rather than to more orthodox climbing that he devoted himself.

President of the Alpine Club, editor of the *Alpine Journal*, Stephen spread his influence over the mountain world not only by his energy, not only by the force of his personality and the doughtiness of his deeds, but also by his ability to write. *The Playground of Europe*, his book which was published in 1871 and told of his most famous ascents, was not merely the best-written book of Alpine climbing that had been published. It had one quality which all the others, with the exception of Whymper's *Scrambles*, notably lacked. It explained an attitude to life. It was, in the literal sense, literature, which the Oxford Dictionary defines as "writings esteemed for beauty of form or emotional effect". It had not only a lasting influence but a finish beside which almost all other Alpine books that men could then buy had the polish of a crusty loaf.

Stephen did not climb on into old age. Work overtook him like night falling on a traveller hurrying for home. Yet until the last he retained an affection for all the memories that were summoned up by the two old ice-axes he gave to the Alpine Club a few months before his death. "Those quaint old poles", he wrote to Lord Conway, on whose shoulders was falling something of Stephen's mantle at the turn of the century, "reminded me of some of the pleasantest days of my life."

Chapter Six

WHYMPER, THE MAN WITH THE CHIP ON HIS SHOULDER

Sooner or late—in earnest or in jest—
(But the stakes are no jest) Ithuriel's Hour
Will spring on us, for the first time, the test
Of our sole unbacked competence and power
Up to the limit of our years and dower
Of Judgment—or beyond. But here we have
Prepared long since our garland or our grave
For, at that hour, the sum of all our past,
Act, habit, thought and passion, shall be cast
In one addition, be it more or less,
And as that reading runs so shall we do;
Meeting, astounded, victory at the last,
Or, first and last, our own unworthiness.
And none can change us though they die to save!

RUDYARD KIPLING

AS the stately if somewhat ponderous procession of Victorian mountaineers gathered numbers there suddenly burst upon it the young, enthusiastic, and slightly brash figure who was to provide its climax, was to cast over it a rather sultry shadow of doom, and who was to remain, for nearly a century, one of the most written-about, if not the most controversial, figure of the whole astonishing group.

His name was Edward Whymper. He was an artist-engraver, a man who had learned the business in his father's Lambeth works and who, judged by the standards of those who formed the bulk of Alpine Club members, might almost have been dismissed by the one word "trade". It was not that there existed, as such, any distinction of class or money; it was merely that few men of the trading layer of society had the opportunity for making high Alpine ascents.

Whymper's "trade", however, was the direct reason for his first visit to the Alps and, indirectly, for the speed with which he rocketed into the most distinguished parts of the Alpine firmament. At the age of twenty, before setting out for a long tour on behalf of his father's business, he was asked by William Longman to prepare a series of sketches for the coming volume of *Peaks, Passes and Glaciers* which was then in course of preparation. The Pelvoux in the Dauphiné, it was added, was one of those mountains which it was especially desired to illustrate in the volume. The young Whymper, whose imagination had earlier been aroused by the search for Franklin which had stirred the mid-1850's, had long nourished an ambition for Arctic travel. Here, he well reasoned, was the chance for serving at least a near-apprenticeship; in the snow and ice regions of the Alps he might learn something of the problems he would have to overcome. He gladly accepted Longman's commission.

The story of what happened during the following five years is among the most famous of all adventure stories. How the young man made his first Alpine tour almost as a business trip; how some attraction drew him back the following year when he made his first attempt to climb the unclimbed Matterhorn—the mountain whose remarkable form he had not even noted when he had first walked up the valley to Zermatt; how attempt followed attempt until, in 1865, he finally climbed the peak; and how, after the moment of triumph, day was turned into night by the disaster which killed four of the seven members of the party—all these events have become something more than the facts in a story which has moved thousands of men and women who have never climbed a mountain and never wished to do so. They have become more than the climax of the Golden Age of mountaineering. They have become, in some subtle way, the epitome of all mountain-climbing; a moral to those who would argue against the pastime and an inspiration to those who maintain that it leads men not only to higher but also to better things. They have formed the subject of films, of radio plays, books, and a whole wealth of learned papers debating the minutiae of the case, the attraction of which would remain even were there not, to this day, a lingering suspicion; a suspicion that all has not even yet been told about the events of that fateful day in 1865 when the "sharp-eyed lad ran into the Monte Rosa Hotel saying that he had seen an avalanche on the Matterhorn"—an awful avalanche whose import only those on the mountain then knew.

There are two reasons for this enduring interest in Whymper and the main event of his life. One lies in the story of the Matterhorn itself, the second in the character of its conqueror.

Whymper climbed for none of the mixed moral reasons that moved his contemporaries. He saw mountains clearly and without qualification as a challenge to man's supremacy. He climbed, it must be admitted, for a reason entirely the reverse of those which affected most of the men who formed the Alpine Club. It must be wondered whether he ever understood any of them.

Whymper makes icily clear in the fourth chapter of the *Scrambles* just what it was that attracted him to the Matterhorn. The mountain had not been climbed; neither had the Weisshorn, and it is just those two peaks which excited his imagination. When he heard rumours that the Weisshorn had been climbed his interest in it abated. So far as he was concerned, and whatever else he might put into his mountain training, it was then only the Matterhorn that was really important. This single-mindedness is underlined in a letter which Hort wrote to his wife from Switzerland on August 1, 1865. He had been in touch with Girdlestone, who had himself been with Whymper only a few days before the accident, and Hort says of Whymper: "He was resolved to do the Matterhorn, and equally resolved, when that was done, to give up mountaineering, because there were no more *new* great mountains to be conquered."

Whymper *had* to climb the Matterhorn—not when he first saw it, for the sheer wonder of its form appears to have passed him by, but when he first appreciated that his long limbs, stamina, and energy enabled him to climb and climb well. Here, in this large lump of stone was an object that had so far defied the progress of the age in which he lived; as a matter of duty it had to be conquered.

The attitude was hardly a happy one and from the moment of decision the tragedy of Whymper's story somehow appears inevitable. It is true that on the bare facts as told by Whymper there seemed nothing inevitable about it. He might never have succeeded in climbing the mountain. There might never have been the plans of a party of Italians, plans which matured in the summer of 1865 so that they were trying to climb the mountain, with Carrel, Whymper's former guide, while his party was on the mountain. A dozen events might have intervened but, reading the *Scrambles*, one cannot feel that they were likely. Events marched steadily forward as Whymper's experience increased, and as he made his second, third, fourth, fifth, sixth, and seventh attempts to climb the mountain. When it might have been ascended by other parties—and Tyndall's was one that nearly did so—Fate steps in with upraised hand; she brings the Italian expedition to Breuil at the right moment, gives Whymper time to hurry across the Theodule Pass, brings up Hadow, Hudson, and Lord Francis Douglas, and sets the stage for the final scene. It is this sense of inevitable doom, spreading over a whole life from the moment that Whymper decides that the mountain shall be his and his alone, as much as the story of the accident itself, which gives a certain tragic dignity to Whymper's story.

This is heightened by the fact that Whymper's philosophy, which drove him up and on to the mountain, did not quite stand up to the accident. Many men who had sought some mystic revelation in the mountains continued, not only to climb but to preach the value of the hills, even after friends and relatives had perished. Whymper, who climbed to prove man's supremacy, not only gave up high climbing after the accident—as he had, in any case, planned to do—but looked at the world through different eyes. For him there was "never glad confident morning again".

The accident formed a watershed in Whymper's life. It formed a dividing line, marking a deep contrast not only in the things that he did but also in the kind of man into which he was developing; twenty-five was a young age at which to have crossed it.

Until that day in 1865 everything had gone relatively well with him. The Matterhorn had been the only major mountain on which he had been repeatedly repulsed. His reputation had grown season by season, and it must have seemed that in spite of his background, in spite of the fact that he had an approach to climbing very different from that of his contemporaries, in spite of his naturally dour and unfriendly nature, the place he was to take in the select Alpine circle would be an important one. It was, in fact, destined to be unique. After the accident a cloud seemed to hang over everything that he did. It is true that he became a member of the Alpine Club Committee for two years. After the publication of the *Scrambles* he was Vice-President. He went to the Andes, and he achieved one of his early ambitions by visiting Greenland. Yet nothing except the business of earning a living appears to have moved him as climbing moved him between the ages of twenty and twenty-five. It may be, as Hort suggested, that the passion died when "there were no more *new* great mountains to be conquered". It is certain that the first fine careless rapture had not been transmuted into the calmer but more abiding emotion which lights the middle and later life of so many mountaineers; instead, all joy had gone from the business and life was darker and more empty because of it.

Whymper's first tour of the Alps was a seven-week affair which in 1860 took him to the Oberland, to Zermatt, and to Chamonix. He made a number of minor ascents, crossed a number of passes, some of them alone, and, as he said, acquired the passion for mountain-scrambling. He was agile, active, audacious, and impatient of all authority. It was typical that when he arrived at Chamonix and found the Mer de Glace closed to tourists for the visit of the Emperor Napoleon, he should have scrambled above the glacier, outwitted the guards, and arrived at the Montanvert as the Imperial party was leaving. The same afternoon, he adds, he failed to get to the Jardin, and very nearly succeeded in breaking a leg.

The next year he went back to the Alps with one main aim, to climb Mont Pelvoux which had been unsuccessfully attempted the previous year by Bonney and his party. As usual, Whymper succeeded. He met Reginald Macdonald, a young clerk in the Colonial Office, made with him the first ascent of the peak and then, after ten days' wandering, crossed the Mont Cenis, where the great tunnel was in course of construction, and made his first attempt on the Matterhorn.

It was on this occasion that he had his first meeting with Jean-Antoine Carrel, the Italian guide who regarded the Matterhorn as his own domain, and whose ambition it was to make the ascent from Italy for the honour of his native valley.

By 1861 there had been more than one attempt on the Matterhorn; the majority of mountaineers still considered that it was not only inaccessible but that it would remain so. Carrel himself had made tentative attempts with other men from his little village of Breuil, below the southern slopes of the Matterhorn, and had eventually reached the "Chimney", a prominent feature 12,650 ft. up the mountain, and 2,132 ft. below the summit. In 1860, the three Parker brothers, Liverpool business men whose promise of meteoric Alpine careers came to little, tackled the Matterhorn without guides from Zermatt, following, so far as they went, roughly the route by which the mountain was eventually climbed five years later. Francis Vaughan Hawkins, a barrister who had been climbing since the mid-1850's, had reconnoitred the Matterhorn in 1859 with Bennen, a guide from the Valais, and one of the few other than Carrel who believed that the mountain would one day be climbed. In 1860 Bennen, together with Jean-Jacques Carrel—uncle of Jean-Antoine—and Professor Tyndall, had climbed some 300 ft. beyond the "Chimney". In 1861, the Parkers had renewed their attempts from the Zermatt side, but had climbed only slightly beyond the point they had reached the previous year.

This was the position when Whymper arrived at Breuil with an unnamed guide and negotiated for the services of Carrel, "the cock of the valley", the "well-made resolute-looking fellow with a certain defiant air". Sparks flew, Whymper attacked the mountain with his inexperienced guide but without Carrel, and from the evening light of a bivouac watched two figures creep past—Carrel and his uncle stealing a march on the foreigners and trying to ensure that the first ascent should be made not only from the Italian side but also by Italians. It was possibly from that moment that the scales tipped over, that what had been a desire to be first on the summit of the Matterhorn became an almost pathological obsession with Whymper.

On this occasion Whymper was turned back below the "Chimney". Carrel climbed higher, up to that spot where he had previously used the iron spike of his axe to cut in the living rock the date, a cross, his initials, and the rough design of a tiara.

Whymper returned to England, the idea of Alpine conquest as deeply engraved on his mind as Carrel's cross had been cut into the rock of the Matterhorn. He was elected a member of the Alpine Club. He brooded over his defeat on the mountain, and the following season he returned to Switzerland earlier than before, during the first days of July. He made his second and third attempts on the Matterhorn, both with Macdonald, went up Monte Rosa, and then made his fourth attempt on the Matterhorn—an attempt made alone, and one during which he climbed past the points reached by earlier explorers, to a height of about 13,400 ft. During the descent he sustained the dramatic fall which is the subject of a famous illustration in the *Scrambles*, an illustration whose suggestion of a near-vertical drop of 200 ft. has a bearing on a later dispute about another illustration in the book. He made a fifth attempt on the mountain the same year and was only prevented from making yet another by the cantankerous argument which broke out between himself and Professor Tyndall.

The following year, 1863, Whymper again visited his old battlefield in the Pennines, attempted the Dent d'Hérens, completed a circuit of the Matterhorn, ascended the Grand Tournalin by making the first ascent of the North-West arête, and then carried out the sixth attempt on the Matterhorn, an attempt which was halted by bad weather.

It was on this occasion that Wilberforce, the Bishop of Oxford, was speaking to a number of Englishmen in the dining-room of the Hôtel Mont Cervin in Zermatt, and referred to the Matterhorn as still unclimbed.

> We all [said one who was there] knew that Whymper was, that very day, making one of his attempts upon the mountain, and I am afraid that bets were freely offered and taken as to whether the Bishop was correct.

Whymper had achieved something of a reputation by this time. He was relentless in his assault on rocks, he used every device which his ingenuity could invent, and he had none of the dislike which existed even then for artificial aids. He designed his own form of grappling iron which could be slung high above the climber in the hope that it might gain a grip on some rock or protuberance above a difficult spot—perhaps the genuine precursor of a delicate climb known as "Rope-Wall" on the Milestone Buttress of Tryfaen in North Wales. He devised the Whymper Tent. He would bar no artifice in his single-minded intention of getting to the top of whatever mountain he chose to attack.

He was, therefore, more than adequately equipped when he set out for his great tour of the Dauphiné in 1864, a tour in whose tracks many mountaineers have followed with admiration not unmixed with wonder. With Moore and Horace Walker he left St. Michel in the Arc Valley, and between the middle and end of June made an elaborate series of magnificent first ascents and passages. The first crossing of the Col des Aiguilles d'Arves, the first ascent of the south peak of the Aiguilles de la Sausse, the first passage of the Brèche de la Meije by which a passage was forced from La Grave on the Route Napoléon to La Berarde, the remote little village lying in the heart of the Dauphiné, the first ascent of the Ecrins, the highest peak in the area, and the first passage of the Col de la Pilatte, were the principal incidents in the amazing fortnight.

All these were expeditions which had excited the interest of more experienced, of older, and of more mature mountaineers. Whymper's party contained, it is true, experienced men in the persons of Moore and Walker; it was led by Croz and Christian

Almer, two of the greatest guides then alive. Yet it is difficult not to believe that the driving force came largely from Whymper, One can see him demanding just that little extra effort; urging, cajoling, ordering, being as ill-tempered as the occasion might demand, and finally getting his own way when the others might have let the sport take its own course.

From the Dauphiné, Whymper went to Chamonix, and with Moore and Adams-Reilly continued to add to his collection of "firsts"—Mont Dolent, the Aiguille de Trelatête, and the Aiguille d'Argentière, as well as the first passages of the Col de Triolet and the Moming Pass.

The following fateful year began in the same way, with first ascents—notably of the Grand Cornier and the Aiguille Verte—and success sprouting from almost every venture that Whymper touched. Then, on July 12, he arrived at Zermatt with Lord Francis Douglas, a climber of some mountaineering, and considerable athletic, reputation whom he had met near Breuil. At Zermatt they encountered Hudson, who was accompanied by Michel Croz and a young man named Hadow whom Hudson was escorting on his first visit to the Alps. Whymper knew that Carrel, his former guide, was about to lead an Italian party in an attempt to reach the summit of the Matterhorn from the Italian side. Almost on the spur of the moment, it seems, Whymper and Lord Francis Douglas linked parties with Hudson and Hadow and decided to make a combined attack on the mountain from Zermatt. On the morning of Thursday the thirteenth, the party set out for the mountain—Whymper, Hudson, Lord Francis Douglas, and Hadow; with, as guides, Croz and "old" Peter Taugwalder; and, as porters, Taugwalder's two sons, one of whom finally stayed with the party until the summit was reached.

The story of the Matterhorn accident has been told and re-told in extensive detail, and it is only necessary to recapitulate the bare bones of the matter. Arrived on the summit—without having encountered any of the major difficulties which had been feared—the party of four amateurs and three guides saw the Italian party many hundreds of feet below, on the southern, Italian, slopes of the mountain. The British party shouted down, waved to the Italians, and even prized out loose boulders which went crashing down the steep face, in an effort to ensure that those below should know of their defeat. There followed an hour of gazing on the summit, of seeing the old peaks from a new and triumphant angle, what Whymper himself has described as "one crowded hour of glorious life".

Whymper and his party moved off from the summit with Croz leading. Behind Croz came the young Hadow, already deeply exhausted by the climb; Hudson; Lord Francis Douglas, and then the elder Taugwalder. Whymper, and "young" Peter Taugwalder who was to be last man on the rope, remained on the summit for a few minutes longer than their companions, then roped together with Whymper in front. Some way below the summit the two joined themselves on to the already lengthy rope of five men.

A few hundred feet down they reached the steepest part of their route. The slabs were dangerous but not inherently difficult, although in the circumstances they must have been difficult enough. At one point, Croz turned to guide Hadow's feet into the best positions on the rocks. Hadow appears to have slipped—although this is still only surmise—and to have knocked Croz from the position where he was standing firm. Their combined weight pulled Hudson from the rocks, and the combined weight of the three men pulled off Lord Francis Douglas.

> Immediately we heard Croz's exclamation, old Peter, and I planted ourselves as firmly as the rocks would permit [says Whymper in the *Scrambles*]. The rope was taut between us, and the jerk came on us both as on one man. We held; but the rope broke mid-way between Taugwalder and Lord Francis Douglas. For a few seconds we saw our unfortunate companions sliding downwards on their backs, and spreading out their hands, endeavouring to save themselves. They passed from our sight uninjured, disappearing one by one, and fell from precipice to precipice on to the Matterhorngletscher below, a distance of nearly 4,000 feet in height. From the moment the rope broke, it was impossible to help them.
>
> So perished our comrades.

This was the disaster whose news swept across Europe and

whose impact was, in the words of Captain Farrar, to set back the sport of mountaineering by a whole generation of men.

There are many factors which combined to give the Matterhorn accident—and which still combine to give it—a unique interest and fascination. The first, of course, was the way in which events had, almost inevitably it appears in retrospect, built themselves up to the tragic climax. Secondly and in some ways even more important, there were the circumstances of the four men who fell to their deaths; they were no ordinary travellers. Charles Hudson was known in the small circle of climbers as possibly the finest amateur of his time; Croz was one of the greatest guides; Hadow, even at the age of nineteen, was acquiring a reputation for athletic endurance even though he had virtually no mountain background; Lord Francis Douglas, young but already experienced, was a man who had a golden future opening out before him while to the Continent at least he represented the dying tradition of the English milord. There were the international repercussions aroused by the obvious rivalry between the British and the Italian parties. And there were the persistent rumours—frequently scandalous and invariably ill-informed—that Whymper was not telling all that he might have told about the early stages of the fateful descent. Any one of these things might have turned the Matterhorn accident into a talking-point; together they turned it into *the* talking-point on which any argument against the practice of mountain-climbing might conveniently be hung.

In addition, there were some interesting technical details of the ascent and the descent. It was an unusual if not unique practice for seven men to be climbing on one rope on a mountain of this difficulty; the inclusion in the party of Hadow was a matter for which Hudson has been criticised more than once; there was the peculiar but easily explainable coincidence that three different types and qualities of ropes were used to link the party together. All these facts combined to make the Matterhorn accident a matter over which climbing men might argue interminably, an endless puzzle of theories and formulae and speculations in which there was enough technical information available to keep the debate within reasonable bounds yet going for ever. Of more general importance was the outcry which the accident aroused.

Newspapers in every country in Europe commented upon the accident in their feature or their leader columns, *The Times* pontifically asking of mountain-climbing in general: "But is it life? Is it duty? Is it common sense?"

Whymper himself, automatically held at Zermatt until the Government enquiry on the accident had been held, regarded the outcry with a contemptuous disdain that is readily understandable. He had given a short account of the affair to the English chaplain at Zermatt who, with Whymper's approval, informed *The Times*. Nothing more, felt Whymper, was really needed of him, although he agreed that he would give a private report of the affair to the Alpine Club. He left Zermatt for Interlaken, was persuaded there to prepare an account of the accident for use by the Swiss and Italian Alpine Clubs, and then returned to England. It was only after he had returned home, and learned of the sensation that the accident had caused, that he finally wrote a fuller account for *The Times*. That account, dated August 7, from his home at Haslemere, was substantially the same as that contained in the *Scrambles*, which was published six years later.

It is now generally accepted that the full story of the Matterhorn disaster has been pieced together with the possible exception of minor and unimportant details. Yet it seems clear that for some reason—possibly the wish to shield one of the six other members of the party—Whymper did not readily reveal all the details of the accident.

Bishop Browne, a Fellow and Lecturer at St. Catherine's College, Cambridge in 1865, was visited by Whymper on his return to England immediately after the accident.

> As Whymper had got into the way of consulting me about matters other than Alpine [he wrote later], I was the first person to whom he gave a full account of what really took place. He came to see me in Cambridge. He had sealed up the bag in which he had the remains of the rope. He came to consult me on two questions of casuistry, on at least one of which he did not take my advice.

It might at first be thought that the reference is merely to minor matters, possibly those elucidated when Captain Farrar succeeded in obtaining publication of the evidence given at the Court of Enquiry held in Zermatt after the accident.

However, some years after the publication of these proceedings Lord Conway of Allington, then the Grand Old Man of climbing, added a footnote to Browne and threw more light on the queer question of the rope. "The late Dr. G. F. Browne, once Bishop of Bristol, who in his turn became President of the Alpine Club, told me not many years ago that he was the only living man who knew the truth about the accident and that the knowledge would perish with him, as it has perished." Then he comes to the rope.

> It happened [he says] that Whymper was the last man in the party and could not actually see Hadow's slip and Croz' overthrow by him, but two or three strands of the rope might have been severed beforehand without anyone knowing. The end of the rope would have retained some sign of the cutting. The end engraved in *Scrambles* is not the one where the breakage occurred. It is the right rope but not the broken end.

Whymper did, in fact, seek more than one adviser when he returned to England in 1865. Oscar Browning says that he went straight to John Cowell, the Secretary of the Alpine Club, and told him the story. "I was in London that day, and Cowell repeated the story to me. The next morning Whymper's narrative appeared in *The Times*, omitting some things which he had told to Cowell."

These "things omitted" may have been the threats which—Whymper alleged in the *Scrambles*, though not in *The Times* letter—had been made to him by the Taugwalders on the latter part of the descent. They may have been merely minor details of interest to mountaineers but of no significance to the general story of the Matterhorn accident.

Whatever the truth, the Matterhorn accident flung its shadow across the Victorian scene as no other had done. The prophets of disaster appeared to have been justified, as was Ruskin who knew the Alpine glory entirely from below. *All the Year Round*, then

20 As a Man of 25

21 In his Middle Fifties

edited by Charles Dickens spoke—through Dickens' mouth, it seems certain—of the

> society for the scaling of such heights as the Schreckhorn, the Eiger, and the Matterhorn [which] contributed about as much to the advancement of science as would a club of young gentlemen who should undertake to bestride all the weathercocks of all the cathedral spires of the United Kingdom.

The mountaineers themselves, so shocked were they by the tragedy, so much did four lives then mean, suffered glumly and largely in silence, knowing that they were right in their own attitude to climbing, but knowing also that the accident had given the rest of the world a stick with which to beat them.

Whymper himself exhibited little emotion, swung his interests from mountain-climbing to the more scientific investigation of the Alps, and set steadily to work on the laborious task of writing, rewriting, and rewriting yet again, the one great book of his life which was to give him an immortality even more sure than that gained by his ascent of the Matterhorn.

In the year following the accident he returned to the Alps to investigate the theory and structure of glaciers. In 1867 he achieved his ambition of exploring Greenland. In 1869 he revisited the Alps, but did little more than cross the Col du Lautaret and revisit the Mont Cenis tunnel, through which, two years later, he made a journey on the first train to traverse the line.

Throughout these years there had been persistent rumours that Whymper's book was about to appear but, as *The Times* was later to say of his volume on the Andes, finally published twelve years after his travels through them, the author seemed to take a grim delight in disappointing the public.

At last, in 1871, there appeared Whymper's *Scrambles amongst the Alps in the Years 1860–1869*. It was an astonishing book, a mixture of naïve amateur writing and inspired phrases, of first-class descriptive reporting and dull slabs that might have been inserted as examples of what to avoid, of scientific comments and purple patches. It was an astonishing book because, in spite of its technical failings, it was a real book in which a man revealed himself; a book, moreover, in which one can still hear the thunder of the falling rocks, and whose power is as strong as it was four-fifths of a century ago.

The *Scrambles* was first produced by Murray at the round Victorian sum of a guinea, and its second edition appeared two years later. A third, slightly abridged, came out in 1879; a fourth in 1893, and a fifth in 1900. A shilling edition with photographs instead of the original illustrations appeared in the blue-bound Nelson library in 1908. And in 1936 there came the new edition from Murray, with photographs, maps, and appendices that included for the first time for popular reading the results of the Zermatt inquest on the accident. The book was translated into French and German, and pirated in other languages from one end of the Continent to the other. It held and retained the affection not only of most mountaineers but of whole generations of potential climbers. Lord Schuster, whose mountain prose, almost alone, can compare with Stephen's, is one of the hundreds who have acknowledged their debt to Whymper for first having aroused their interest in the mountains. The late Frank Smythe is another.

The peculiar fascination of the book does not lie only in the story that it tells. It has an honest artlessness that summons up the picture of Whymper, the man, in a way that few photographs can ever hope to do. It is true that Whymper wrote and rewrote every line innumerable times; it is true that he wrote fresh chapters in some of the later editions and excised some of his earlier material; it is true that he was for ever altering and amending and correcting, and that late in life he admitted to Coolidge that the book still contained many mistakes. Yet in spite of all these things the book yet remained one man's record of the influence that mountains had had on him. For a whole segment of the only partially informed public, Whymper *was* mountaineering for the rest of his life.

The *Scrambles* consolidated Whymper's position as a national figure. He might not be the typical mountaineer; he might not even be a normal one; yet for thousands of men and women this stern-lipped sombre young man of few words was the survivor of the Matterhorn. Whymper had at last found his lonely niche in life. He cultivated the solitude of the position, and there is little reason to believe that he would have been any happier had his relations with his fellow men been more frequent, more normal, or more friendly.

He did not entirely give up mountaineering. In 1872, he made a solitary and rather rambling visit to Greenland. He went back to the Matterhorn again and made the seventy-sixth ascent of the peak with his old friend Jean-Antoine Carrel as guide. Two years later he again visited the mountain, and one cannot help wondering if by this time the Matterhorn had not begun to cast over Whymper some spell which had been ineffective when, as a youth, he had tackled the mountain bull-in-a-china-shop fashion.

Some modified version of the old feelings blazed up at least once more. In 1879 Whymper left England for the Andes of Ecuador, his aim being to discover how men might live and move at great altitudes. The expedition, which he organised and ran almost entirely by himself, was a complete success, just as were almost all the other mountain tasks that he tackled throughout his life. He made the first and then the second ascent of Chimborazo, travelled extensively through the high mountains of Ecuador, and spent more than thirty nights above 14,000 ft. On his return, the Alpine Club held a meeting at the Royal Institution where Whymper lectured to an audience that included Edward VII, then Prince of Wales, duly received the vote of thanks moved by His Royal Highness, and departed to start work on his monumental *Travels amongst the Great Andes of the Equator*.

It was the record of Whymper's last major mountain exploration, an accurate but rather turgid record which lacked all hint of the fire which had blazed up in parts of the *Scrambles*.

Whymper visited the Rockies three times in the early 1900's, but although he made some new ascents on the first of these and opened up much new country, the journeys were overshadowed by his dependence on the Canadian Pacific which had commissioned him for the task. Significantly, he wrote to Coolidge shortly before the third visit, suggesting that the latter "might say something in a suggestive way about the want of a book upon the Rocky Mountains of Canada".

During the last forty years of his life, Whymper's name fails to occur with the frequency which one might expect, either in mountain records or in those which dealt with the sociable meetings of climbers. This must have been all the more galling to his sense of perspective since he knew that he was, for most people, the most famous of all living mountaineers. The audiences which he drew to lectures left no doubt about that.

Yet the cold-shouldering which Whymper appears to have suffered throughout the greater part of his life was not due either to the Matterhorn accident or to his upbringing. It was simply that he was an unclubbable sort of man, a hardly amiable fellow who would go to considerable lengths to ensure that he gained the maximum financial reward for any effort which he expended.

He had, for instance, paid especial tribute in his Andes book to the help which C. E. Mathews had in his typically generous way given him in obtaining the necessary official facilities. Mathews, however, was lecturing on his own experiences in the Alps—lecturing almost entirely to small local societies to whom he willingly volunteered his time and his energies. Whymper, so soon as he learned of this, caused his lecture agent to write to Mathews and bid him discontinue the use of the title "Scrambles in the Alps" for the talks which Mathews was giving to what were virtually small groups of friends and acquaintances. Mathews, in his kindly way, could hardly understand the action. "I have been his friend for twenty-five years", he wrote in amazement to Lord Conway.

During the latter years of his life Whymper lived, almost literally, on the fruits of his explorations, lecturing up and down the country on his Alpine experiences, telling and re-telling the Matterhorn story, writing for the popular magazines, and encouraging in every possible way the sale of the two guide-books which he later wrote on the history and topography of Chamonix and Zermatt.

He was argumentative, jealous of his position, and thin-skinned when it came to criticism. The most famous of all his disputes concerned "Almer's Jump", a jump that has passed into Alpine history and almost became the subject of a libel suit. It had taken place in 1864 when Whymper and his party, accompanied by Christian Almer and Michel Croz, were descending from the summit of the Ecrins, whose first ascent they had just made.

The incident, shown by Whymper in the *Scrambles* in a dramatic full-page illustration, was described by him thus:

> We were on the very edge of the arête. On one side was the enormous precipice facing the Pelvoux, which is not far from perpendicular; on the other a slope exceeding 50 degrees. A deep notch brought us to an abrupt halt. Almer, who was leading, advanced cautiously to the edge on hands and knees, and peered over; his care was by no means unnecessary, for the rocks had broken away from under us unexpectedly several times. In this position he gazed down for some moments, and then, without a word, turned his head and looked at us. His face *may* have expressed apprehension or alarm, but it certainly did not show hope or joy. We learned that there was no means of getting down, and that we must, if we wanted to pass the notch, jump across on to an unstable block on the other side. It was decided that it should be done, and Almer, with a larger extent of rope than usual, jumped. The rock swayed as he came down upon it, but he clutched a large mass with both arms and brought himself to anchor.

The incident passed without comment for more than a quarter of a century after the publication of Whymper's book. Then, in an obituary notice on Christian Almer contributed to the *Year-book of the Swiss Alpine Club*, Coolidge re-described the incident and added a footnote.

> After publication of this book (the *Scrambles*) I immediately showed this picture to Almer [said the explosive note] who then assured me, in all earnest, that he had never done such a thing and would never have been able to do it.

Whymper, went the implication, had invented the whole "jump" story to give colour to his account of the Ecrins ascent.

The trouble was immediately brewed up by both sides with considerable and obvious glee. Whymper wrote to Coolidge. Coolidge reaffirmed his statement. The Alpine Club, the Swiss

Alpine Club, and Horace Walker, the only other member of Whymper's party then living, were all drawn into the argument. Whymper asked for, and was refused, a special meeting of the Alpine Club at which the matter might be thrashed out.

Walker agreed with Whymper's version, and Whymper thereupon threatened a libel action. Coolidge refused to withdraw his statement and wrote to Tuckett—who was trying to play mediator between the two men and being soundly criticised by both: "If he worries me much more he will *for that only* be turned out of all foreign A.C.'s. I am far too useful a member to be lost—save in the eyes of A.C."

As to the libel threat, Coolidge added: "He will have some trouble to catch me, an 'alien' living in a foreign land, for a paragraph published in a foreign land." Finally, Whymper dropped the libel threat—and circulated to all members of the Alpine Club a sixteen-page booklet which included a reproduction of the contested illustration and a generous selection of the letters that had followed the outbreak of the argument.

The fairest summing-up of the whole incident came a few years later in a letter from Captain Farrar to Coolidge.

> I do not think W. *invented* the incident [he said]. Remember he became a noted man through the Matterhorn affair. He was writing his first book, which was looked for by the public, and was expected to be sensational. What more natural than that a clever draughtsman should use some little incident to make a sensational picture and unconsciously exaggerate? We are all human. And who on earth in those early days ever expected the minute criticism to which nowadays Alpine matters are, in the fierce light of completed knowledge, exposed? God help all those early authors and I thank God that my own very few and far between literary efforts are written with a determination to make them deadly true if deadly dry.

It was an apt comment on an argument that might, between any other two men, have been solved with a little common sense and a little courtesy. Neither Whymper nor Coolidge had much of either.

Yet Whymper was not, as is often imagined, perpetually at

loggerheads with the scholar, ten years his junior, who criticised in detail so much of his work. The two men corresponded freely and at times affectionately from 1878 until Whymper's death in 1911, Whymper himself freely admitting to Coolidge much that he would have denied in public.

> In the second edition [of the *Scrambles*] several illustrations were added; and the text was revised. A great many corrections were made (too numerous to be pointed out). Some were printers' blunders, others were author's faults. In the fourth edition, I have endeavoured to lessen both printers' blunders and author's faults.

There appears, in fact, to have been a good deal of confession between the two of them.

The friendship even recovered from the discussion of Almer's Leap. Early in the new century Whymper was again writing to Coolidge, and Coolidge was inviting him to the Chalet Montana, his home in Grindelwald, the village to which he had moved in 1896. "When I come, I shall come in the old style," wrote Whymper, then in his seventies. "Shall walk up, not order rooms in advance, and take my chance as to finding a room. If none can be had, I shall camp out."

Finally, he did come, in the hot summer of 1911, sending from Geneva and Zermatt a series of cards, written in a quavering unsteady hand, warning Coolidge when to expect him. He arrived on the morning of September 3, and for nearly a day conqueror and chronicler of the Alps talked together.

It would be interesting to speculate on what passed between the two men who, between them, had seen the passage of so much Alpine history, who had seen the sport of climbing transformed from the quiet passion of the few into a pastime attracting its thousands, a pastime with its own clubs and traditions and extensive literature.

It seems likely that in spite of their notorious feuds they bore one another little permanent ill-will. The extensive correspondence between them suggests, in fact, that each may really have enjoyed the occasional practise of an engagement with someone as irascible as himself; that each may have felt some sympathy for an opponent who had as few friends as himself.

Whymper left Coolidge toward evening, travelled to Zermatt, then to Geneva and on to Chamonix where he took a room. He fell ill, refused all aid, and was dead within a few days.

Chapter Seven

COOLIDGE, THE BOSWELL OF THE ALPS

I seek and desire
Even as the wind
That travels the plain
And stirs in the bloom
Of the apple-tree.

I wander through life,
With the searching mind
That is never at rest,
Till I reach the shade
Of my lover's door.

SAPPHO

THE ascent of the Matterhorn, even if it had not been accompanied by tragedy, might easily have brought to an end the driving force behind the sport of climbing which was developing so vigorously. It might easily have stultified, beyond hope of salvation, the growing interest in mountain-climbing for the peak was, with the exception of the Meije in the Dauphiné, the last great unclimbed summit of the Alps. The fearful accident which befell the conquerors—an accident which in the eyes of many was caused by the just and avenging finger of Fate wiping its relentless finger down the slate—did, of course, cast a gloom over the years which immediately followed. Yet neither the ascent of the mountain, nor the accident on the descent, permanently crippled the advance of climbing.

The reason for the continuation and ultimate resurgence of mountaineering after 1865 lay simply in the one fact that men did find in it something more satisfying than mere physical conquest. Just as a Christian can understand a resurrection beyond the grave, so could a large number of Victorians see, beyond the Matterhorn disaster, a continuing rightness about mountaineering. They realised that it was an occupation or even a belief which could satisfy all manner of unexpected demands in a man. It might even satisfy the intellectual demands of a scholar who could see, in the unploughed field of Alpine history, a whole life's work waiting to be done.

The best example of this was that most peculiar of all Victorian mountaineers, W. A. B. Coolidge, who first visited Switzerland in the August of 1865 at the age of fifteen with his aunt, Miss Meta Brevoort. On that occasion the boy sent back to his mother from Zermatt the carefully engraved note-paper of the hotel on which the Matterhorn was shown, adding that "the two dots you see on the picture represent where they (the victims) fell from, and where they fell. A horrible distance." This alert, communicative correspondent was a weak, slightly pampered, and rather precocious child whom emotional bad luck and an iron will were to transform, during the succeeding fifty years, into the most dominating of Alpine personalities.

It is somewhat surprising that Coolidge, born near New York in 1850 and brought to Europe by his aunt because of his poor health, ever became a mountaineer at all. He was short, leaning to plumpness even in early years; he had a rare facility for picking up and nurturing whatever disease was in range, while even as a youth his sight was so bad that a breaking of the binocle through which he looked at great Alpine views was a major disaster. Yet, short as he was both of stature and of breath, it was of Coolidge that Captain Farrar once said that "it would be as ridiculous for a man to speak of Alpine matters without mentioning the name of Coolidge, as it would be to discuss the Bible without mentioning God".

Farrar was making no overstatement. For at that time—when Coolidge, in one of his periodic disputes with the Alpine Club was breathing fire and destruction on anyone who dared print his name in the *Alpine Journal*—he had not only been editor of the *Journal* for ten years, a member of the Club Committee, and an honorary member of the Club for yet another decade. He had made more than 1,700 mountaineering expeditions, including 600 *grandes courses*; he had, with Lord Conway, edited the first great series of climbing guides to the Alps; he had published score upon score of articles, books, guides, and notes in which every aspect of the Alps was listed, scrutinised, and criticised in a detail and with an accuracy that made comment difficult. He had become the greatest Alpine historian that the world had ever known.

Coolidge had realised, early in life, that no one had yet applied to the history of the Alps and their conquest by man, the same scholarly scrutiny and investigation which had been lavished on so many other obscure and esoteric subjects. Remedying this defect, filling this lacuna in man's knowledge became, as he grew older, the whole aim and object of his life. His standards were high and inflexible, their enforcement almost pathological. On one occasion he condemned a whole book because the author had let slip one wrong accent. When one of his own learned volumes appeared, an alpine journal decided that Coolidge was the only man alive who had the knowledge to review it adequately; he did so—and pointed out with scorn a number of minor errors which the author had made.

The bare facts of Coolidge's life suggest that he was a man cast in no normal mould. Brought as a boy to Europe, he never returned to the United States and when, during the First World War, he was refused a passport both by Britain and by the United States was proud to boast of himself as "the first displaced person". Due to his mother's bad health he was put in the care of his aunt, a woman with whom all his early Alpine wanderings were made, with whom he existed on terms whose intimacy it is a little difficult to understand, and whose early death injected a sullen bitterness into his life which never completely left him. A Fellow, Junior Dean, and later Librarian of Magdalen, he was ordained in 1882, held the honorary curacy of South Hinksey, outside Oxford, for twelve years; and in 1896 retired to Grindelwald where he became first "the sage" and later a legend within his own lifetime.

He is remarkable not only for what he did, but for why he did it, and for the fact that his climbing enthusiasm arose when it did For there was, as he says, a

> sort of palsy that fell upon the good cause after that frightful cata- strophe of July 14, 1865, particularly amongst English climbers Few in numbers, all knowing each other personally, shunning th public as far as possible (and in those days it *was* possible to do so) they went about under a sort of dark shade, looked on with scarcel disguised contempt by the world of ordinary travellers.

Yet in spite of disabilities added by both nature and events Coolidge climbed continuously and strenuously for most of hi active life.

His career, and the factors and events which forced it along it austere but almost predestined path, divide into four parts. Ther is, first, the period of early Alpine wanderings with Miss Brevoort Coolidge being then a boy who lacked any overwhelmin interest in the mountains. There is, secondly, the period whic started in 1870 with his first visit to the Dauphiné, a period durin which he travelled on major expeditions through the Alps wit his aunt. There is the period of semi-bibliographical exploratio that followed her death in 1876. And there is the last long perio which started when Coolidge moved to Grindelwald in 1896 an which ended only with his death in 1926.

The young nephew who crossed the Strahlegg Pass in 186 passing Herr Baedeker "the guide-book gentleman", wh ascended the Cima di Jazzi, crossed the Theodule and the Col d Géant, all with his aunt, drew from her enthusiasm for the Alpin world some unfiltered essence that was to dominate his life. H was happy about the domination. He was a willing hero-wor shipper and there can be little doubt that it was his abnorm affection for her which drove him up into the heights, largely metaphorically at the end of her ice-axe. Her presence gave hin it appears, a new confidence which his own physical disabiliti must have made doubly pleasant.

In 1867 and 1868, they were back again. On the secon occasion they had engaged Christian Almer, a guide then at th height of his fame. He had been employed before the Coolidg

Zermatt & le Mont Cervin.
Valais.

Aosta Sunday morning
Sept 24th 1865

Dear mamma I have not written to you for a long time and I am very much ashamed. I went to the Hörnli alone on Monday and came back by the Zmutt Glacier. It was a beautiful view but a very hard climb. Tuesday we went to the hotel on the Riffel on ~~horse~~ mule back and aunty continued up to the Gorner Grat on ~~horse~~ mule back but I left my mule at the Riffel hotel and walked up. The view is very fine but ~~it~~ the way is all over rocks. Wednesday aunty's foot being better we went up the Cima di Jazi. The way is all over the snow and ice. We met a party of two young men English

With much love I am yr Willy

Love to Maud I hope your foot is better

3 A Letter from W. A. B. Coolidge to his Mother following his first visit to Zermatt at the age of 15, in 1865

24 Miss Brevoort

25 W. A. B. Coolidge

TSCHINGEL'S PEAKS AND PASSES.

1865.

Torrenthorn.
Tschingel Pass.

1868.

Blümlis Alps.
Balmhorn.
Nesthorn.
Mönchjoch.
Aletschhorn

1869.

Grands Mulets.
Aiguille de Miage.
Col de Bérenger (1st passage.)
Col du Mont Tondu.
Grand Combin.
Breithorn.
Monte Rosa.

1870.

Col des Aiguilles d'Arve
Diablerets.
Brünegghorn.

1871.

Eiger.
Jungfrau (from Wengern Alp.)
Alphübeljoch.
Triftjoch.
Fusshorn (1st ascent.)

1872.

Brèche de la Meije.
Col de la Tempe.
Aletschhorn (crossed.)
Strahleck.
Mönch (from Wengern Alp.)
Jungfraujoch (descent to Wengern Alp.)
Finsteraarhorn.
Agassizjoch.
Finsteraarjoch.
Wetterhorn.
Doldenhorn.

1873.

Aiguille d'Arve (lowest peak, 1st ascent.)
Col de la Lauze.
Râteau (1st ascent.)
Col des Ecrins.
Col du Glacier Blanc.
Grande Ruine (1st ascent)
Col de la Casse Deserte (1st passage.)
Col de la Pilatte (descent to Vallouise.)

1874.

Col du Tour
Mont Pourri.
Pic de la Grave (1st ascent.)
Brèche de St. Christophe.
Ochsenhorn.
Ochsenjoch.

1875.

Klein Schreckhorn.
Brèche de Valsenestre.
Col du Vallon (1st passage)
Pointe de Marguérite (1st ascent.)
Les Berches.
Col des Chamois (1st passage.)
Mont Blanc.

1876.

Fusshörner (1st ascent of 2nd Peak.)

26, 27 Tschingel, and (*left*) the Printed List of her Peaks and Passes

engagement by Hereford George, who had been unable to tackle the Finsteraarhorn as planned, and who had therefore released his guide earlier than was expected.

Almer turned up before time.

> He can't speak a word of either French or English, nor yet understand [Miss Brevoort wrote to her sister]. We immediately unpacked the dictionary and went to work talking. His son ("young" Christian) had, I suppose, broken the news of the "Dame" to him, for he expressed no astonishment but sensibly remarked that he could soon tell after a day's walk with us what and how we could go. He is a short little man with an honest intelligent face, and very communicative.

The meeting was an important one. Under Almer, Coolidge and his aunt were to begin their serious mountaineering together; the links between the Almer family and Coolidge were to last for more than half a century. They climbed the Wetterhorn. They attempted the Finsteraarhorn and the Eiger, and on their repulse from the latter Coolidge was presented with the immortal dog Tschingel, who was to accompany him and his aunt on so many Alpine excursions. The following year they climbed Mont Blanc, unwittingly making the first known *descent* by the Bosses du Dromedaire. They made a whole series of first-class ascents, and by the end of the season had already begun to found that legend of "the young American who climbs with his aunt and his dog".

It is the following year that Coolidge, now twenty, first appears fully formed, out of the chrysalis, a man, a climber, and a planner all in his own right. He had not only served an apprenticeship on the mountains by this time but had seen that apprenticeship acknowledged. Notes to the *Alpine Journal* had been accepted and in February he had been elected a member of the Club. In addition, he had three things of great value to any man wishing to attempt mountaineering in the heroic manner; the master, the companion, and the task.

The master was Tuckett. Coolidge had first written to him at the age of seventeen, cautiously at first, and then with requests for advice on half a hundred mountain matters from bootmakers to aneroids. He had gratefully borrowed equipment which Tuckett had generously offered; finally, the elder man had become what Coolidge called his "Alpine godfather" by proposing him for the Club and guiding him through the necessary formalities which membership entailed. Coolidge had been an enthusiastic, not to say persistent admirer, swamping Tuckett with letters, sometimes twenty or more a month and asking, towards the end of 1869, for advice on what appears to have been his first literary project. He received a somewhat cold reply.

> A *complete* list of all first ascents of mountains 10,000 ft. and upwards would doubtless be interesting but it would involve immense labour [Tuckett pointed out] and, I fear, expose the compiler to the risk of being taken to task for the almost invisible mistakes which questions of priority invariably involve.

There is something ironically amusing about the young Coolidge being chided against the possibility of making "the almost invisible mistakes" whose detection was later to become his speciality. Coolidge was undeterred by Tuckett's coolness and throughout the winter of 1869–1870 there continued a flow of almost daily letters from the enthusiastic youth, then at Oxford, to the firmly established gentleman who early in 1870 invited the young man down to his house near Bristol.

As his companion, Coolidge had his aunt, twenty-five years his senior, a woman of great determination and some eccentricity who was, surprisingly maybe, an ideal companion for her ambitious nephew. It was she, writing to him in 1876, who made what must have been one of the first serious suggestions that Mount Everest might be attempted.

Coolidge's task, as he saw it in the early seventies, was the exploration of the Dauphiné, where he was subsequently to make more than 250 ascents, many dozens of them new. This last great area of unclimbed peaks in Europe, was in those days in much the same condition as that in which Bonney had found it a decade previously.

"I am not quite sure what it was that made us choose Dauphiné as our battleground," says Coolidge, "but I believe it was ambition.

There was a whole world to explore there and that was enough for us." There was, by this time, an "us" about the matter. Coolidge, after years of travelling with, and being mastered by, his aunt, had suddenly become master himself. He rises, for a moment, in real though rather curious stature, and it is from this moment that his great Alpine career really begins to flower.

The choice of area might have been different had he been born even ten years earlier. But during the decade which began in 1860, while Whymper was capturing virgin peaks with an ease never to be known in Europe again, the Alps shrunk immeasurably. The Ultima Thule of the earlier Alpine world had become the "new centre" of Coolidge's day, and he was therefore driven south of the arc into the queer rough land that he was to make peculiarly his own.

It is interesting to compare Whymper and Coolidge, both stepping on to the Alpine stage at the age of twenty, both reaching their own predetermined ends, yet one becoming the most famous of all mountaineers while the other remained, in spite of his unique accomplishments, almost unknown outside a limited circle. The backgrounds to their lives were entirely different. It was not only that by Coolidge's day it was frequently more difficult to confirm that a peak was unclimbed than it was to make the ascent. There was one far more significant difference in the Alpine worlds in which they made their débuts. When Whymper set out on his first journey to make sketches for Mr. Longman, mountaineering was at last beginning to justify itself as a respectable occupation for the eminent Victorians. All Coolidge's early campaigns were carried out during the aftermath of the great accident.

There was also the different social status of the two men, a difference which would not have been so noticeable today. Even Whymper's addresses—they included Lambeth and lodgings in Teddington—have a slightly more proletarian ring than those of the young boy who at the age of twenty had lived in Concord, Guernsey, Paris, and Oxford. Whymper, the artist from the engravers, won the respect of the small circle of men who climbed regularly, the few for most of whom money was rarely a worry; he never became one of them. Coolidge dropped naturally into that leisured society of carriages, servants, and select musical evenings. He was an American, it is true, and at times, he must have appeared a rather unusual specimen to his London friends; yet he had the essential background, the permanent confidence of the man who will never have to work for his living, and he took his place easily and without surprise in the calm assured world of such men as Conway, Freshfield, Tuckett, and Baillie-Grohman. Both Coolidge and Whymper would have preferred life to treat them differently, and the letters of their later years suggest how both of them had their regrets—Coolidge that he had not been born a little earlier, Whymper that he had not been born into a family which would have given him the background to meet Coolidge's certain, constant, and often insupportable assertion that he alone could be right.

Yet if there were these differences of circumstance between the two men, there were also similarities of character and ambition which probably lay at the root of the persistent guerrilla war between them—a war interlarded with long periods of friendship. With each, to be first was the great affair—first on the mountain or first in the recording of its definitive history. For each, one great peak had a fascination which was almost that of the supernatural; when Coolidge wrote of the Meije his writing trembled, as it rarely did, on the verge of inspiration, bringing to his sentences a hint of that troublesome longing that Edward Whymper felt for the Matterhorn. Psychologically, both men came from the same mould; both paid a dear penalty for success, and the accident on the Matterhorn which so affected Whymper's life was only a swifter example of that retribution which slowly overtook Coolidge as his Alpine studies divorced him more surely, year by year, from the lives of other men and women.

In 1870, however, coming events cast no shadow upon Coolidge's decision to devote the opening weeks of his Alpine campaign, as many men have done since, to retracing at least some parts of the journey which Whymper, Moore, and Walker had made through the Dauphiné six years earlier, and in climbing a number of the peaks which their hurried passage had left unclimbed. He had borrowed a number of the original sketches which Tuckett had made of the area in 1862; together with Miss Brevoort, he had gained a brief glimpse of Moore's *Alps in 1864*, then only privately printed, and both of them had read Bonney's *Outline Sketches in the High Alps of Dauphiné*. There was little else that dealt with mountaineering in the area—the *Scrambles* was not published until 1871—and when Coolidge set out from his mother's home in Paris in the summer of 1870 he had justifiable hopes of starting a career as a genuine pioneer.

It was a queer trio which drove through the streets from Mrs. Coolidge's house to take their places in the express to the South. Except for Coolidge's axe—Miss Brevoort never carried one, preferring the long wooden baton which one associates with the early prints of Mont Blanc—it would have been difficult to identify them as mountaineers.

Miss Brevoort was slow-moving and, it must be imagined, a little ponderous in the thick and voluminous clothes with which she ceaselessly experimented but which she was unable to convert satisfactorily to mountaineering. Coolidge once complained vehemently that she was not, as described by a casual writer, a "grosse holländische-amerikanische Miss" but was, on the contrary, "slight and tall". Both writers appear to have been extremists.

Coolidge seemed even less of a mountaineer than his aunt, the complete contrast to Martin Conway, the *beau idéal* of a slightly later period, whose tall figure, flowing hair, and fine moustachios combined with his dual reputation as an art critic and a mountaineer, and created about him an air which would have been theatrical had it not been for the man himself.

The third member of the party was the small bitch Tschingel, already a veteran in her own quiet way.

In the minor hall of fame which the Victorian mountaineers carefully built for themselves, Tschingel deserves a place of her own. She did, after all, make a total of sixty-six major climbs, as well as about 100 minor ones; she did form the final third of the legendary trio; and she was to become, as Miss Brevoort proudly termed her, the only "Honorary Lady member of the Alpine Club".

Tschingel was by no means the first dog to be taken into the ice-world of the Alps. Marc-Théodore Bourrit, one of the earliest of Alpine writers, travelled in the mountains for six years with his dog. De Saussure invariably travelled with his. Yet it was left to an Englishman to take a dog on the first really high Alpine climb. He was Henry Atkinson who, as was almost demanded at the time, followed up his ascent of Mont Blanc in 1837 with a slim pamphlet describing the experience. In it he gives one of the first descriptions of what a dog thought of the upper world.

> It was a little dog [he says] which belonged to one of the guides, Michael Balmat, which accompanied us the whole day, and was the first dog that ever reached the top of Mont Blanc. He was much affected with drowsiness after we quitted the Grand Plateau, and every time we stopped he tried to lie down on our feet, finding the snow cold. He evinced many tokens of surprise by frequently staring about him, and would make an effort to run very fast and then drop. With regard to his appetite, chicken bones disappeared with an amazing rapidity, but he did not appear to suffer from thirst.

It seems likely that this was the animal described by George Barnard, the artist who copied an account from one of Longman's privately printed books, and who says that the guide wanted to take the dog, but that permission was refused by his party who thought it would be a nuisance.

> Of course, it soon overtook them, though the guide protested that he had ordered it to be tied up [says Barnard]. Well, the dog was a trouble, he got between their legs, and bothered them, and they were obliged to throw him over all the crevasses. He was what is called a Spitz dog, a kind distinguished by a very pointed nose, sharp black eyes, and a tail curling stiffly over the back. The mountain atmosphere had an extraordinary effect on this dog; it made him uncurl his tail! As he went up, this bushy appendage

gradually got straighter and straighter, till at last it hung down behind as straight as a broomstick. No Spitz dog's tail was ever before known to uncurl, and curiously enough as he came down his tail by degrees curled up again as usual.

A later canine climber was the little dog who accompanied Kennedy on many of his Alpine travels in the 1860's, and who made the ascent of the 13,500 ft. Aiguille Verte with her master. She disliked some of the hard snow slopes, Kennedy reported, but persevered on to the top and then went to sleep on a rucksack while everyone else admired the view.

Yet all the mountaineering dogs of which records have survived are faint shadows compared with the incomparable Tschingel who for nine glorious seasons rollicked across the Alps with Coolidge and his aunt.

Tschingel has been variously described—a bull terrier, a small bloodhound, a large beagle. She was 1 foot 7 inches high, and she had a brown silky coat with white breast, stomach, stockings and muzzle, and very large brown eyes. Her favourite drinks on the mountain were very human—red wine or weak tea—while although she understood English, German and the dialect of the Canton Valais in Switzerland, she never responded to French. Coolidge always maintained that this was due to her decided views about the Franco-Prussian War which in 1870 involved her in an arduous journey across Europe when she travelled home to Britain with her owners.

Tschingel was born in the spring of 1865, in a small village in the Bernese Oberland, and little is known of the first few months of her life. The following September, however, she was frisking in front of her home when Christian Almer passed by, liked the look of the small dog, bought her for ten francs, and induced her to follow him on foot.

Almer was on his way to join George, and join him he did—together with the dog who trotted up steps cut in a steep ice-slope to meet the party and "excited the admiration of all the spectators by the unconcerned way in which he trotted up the slope". The mistake about the sex of the animal was one that was only tardily corrected; Miss Brevoort stubbornly continued to speak of Tschingel as "he", long after the animal had produced more than thirty puppies.

At the end of Almer's engagement with George in the autumn of 1865, Tschingel—named after the first glacier pass that she crossed—was taken back to the guide's home in Grindelwald, and there the story of her mountaineering might well have ended. Three years later, however, Coolidge and his aunt were turned back by bad weather on the Eiger; and, to lessen Coolidge's disappointment—he was only eighteen at the time—Almer made him a present of Tschingel. The same year she began her main Alpine wanderings, travelling with the Coolidge party on all except the most difficult climbs.

Tschingel was taken to and from the Alps in a specially built travelling box. On the mountains themselves, she usually trotted along as one of the party. Sometimes a rope would be looped through her workaday collar, and she then became physically linked to the people on either side of her. Her paws sometimes bled, but that did not appear to worry her, and she kicked off the special leather boots which Coolidge had made for her.

Like many other dogs, she was particularly good at finding her way across thickly crevassed glaciers, and on at least one occasion helped to find the way home when the guide had lost it; an ability which some scientists explain by the fact that a dog's super-sensitive nose can "scent" the old air that comes up through the crevasses from the depths of the glacier. Writing to her sister of Tschingel, Miss Brevoort explains how the party once crossed the Grindelwald Glacier and adds:

> In one place, we had to cross a very rotten-looking and pretty long snow bridge, but by stretching a rope along it and going one by one (Tschingel was tied and walked along it alone quite solemnly) we got safely over.

Tschingel climbed the Jungfrau, and a number of other well-known summits, but Mont Blanc was probably her most famous climb, for it had always been suspected that the dog which went with the Atkinson party might have broken the rules and been carried for a short distance. Tschingel certainly went all the way on her own four feet, and when she returned from the

28 W. A. B. Coolidge (*left*) and Albert, his manservant, at the Chalet Montana, Grindelwald, in 1920

E. Lewis Lloyd
M. Straton

summit in 1875 a special cannon was fired at Chamonix in her honour.

> She trotted into the village with her head erect and her tail wagging, immensely proud of herself [Miss Brevoort wrote to her sister]. The next day, lying luxuriously on a sofa in the hotel drawing-room she held a kind of state reception which was attended by several hundred persons, including all the guides.

Tschingel never climbed the Matterhorn, although Coolidge had great plans for her to do so in 1876. When his idea matured, he was in one part of the Alps and Miss Brevoort, with Tschingel, was in another. Miss Brevoort needed quite a lot of convincing; finally, she agreed, in principle, that Tschingel could make the ascent to crown her career. But, she added, "I can't bear to think of his doing this without seeing him do it, and as to our going to Zermatt it's not to be thought of, Dear Will, in spite of your economy." Could it not, she implied, be left for another year? Coolidge let the matter rest for that season. Another never came.

As Tschingel grew old, her coat grew white, she became almost blind, and her teeth dropped out. But although she no longer climbed, she still sometimes wore her Sunday-best collar, with its little silver medallions recording all the peaks she had climbed, and the passes she had crossed. Finally in 1879, Coolidge decided that it was kinder to have her put away. The night after he had made the decision, Tschingel died in her sleep before the kitchen fire.

> I am at present in great affliction at the death of my dear old dog Tschingel, which took place on June 16 [Coolidge wrote to C. E. Mathews]. She was so much more a companion than a mere dog that I feel her loss very deeply.

Coolidge never forgot her and when, nearly half a century later, he had another dog, it was a black Newfoundland as dissimilar as possible from Tschingel.

It was some forty years after Tschingel's death that Coolidge was visited in his Grindelwald home by Dr. Monroe Thorington, the great American climber and Alpine historian.

He had his man show me about [Dr. Thorington once said]. And then, just when I was leaving he pointed to the door. There on a hook was Tschingel's collar with the little bangles shining in the sun. Not a word was said, but Coolidge managed something resembling a smile.

In mid- and later life, as Coolidge gathered around himself the impedimenta and glory of an Alpine expert, he was as meticulous about the record of Tschingel as of that of any human being. His letter to one gentleman who had rashly published a short history of the dog without checking with the Master was typical —not only of his attitude to Tschingel but of the whole latter half of his life.

I have only just had time to look at your article on my dog Tschingel [he said] and write at once to *protest very strongly against the remarks you have made as regards my dear aunt, and against the numerous mistakes of fact in this short article.* I supplied you with the printed authentic facts, to which you have paid but little attention. Tschingel *walked* from Kippel up the Torrenthorn, and was not carried. My aunt did *not meet T. on the Torrenthorn*, which she never climbed in all her life, while at the moment of T.'s ascent she was with me near Zermatt. She did not make the 1st ascent of the Jungfrau from the N., but the *first by a woman*. She made the *1st lady's ascent* of the Silberhorn, not the 3rd, our ascent having been the third ever made (Baedeker in 1863 and Hornby and Philpott in 1865 were our only predecessors on the peak). At least two other ladies (Fräulein Brunner of Berne and Miss Walker) had been up the Gr. Schreckhorn before her. *The whole Torrenthorn story is a myth so far as regards my aunt's presence there.* She never saw T. till 1868, and then in H. du Grd. Eiger, here, not in Almer's house which she never visited. The gift of T. was made by Almer *to me*, and took place at a chalet a little above the Hotel at Alpiglen, on this slope of the Kl. Scheidegg. It was to console me for *a failure* on the Eiger (due to verglas on the rocks), a peak which T. never climbed till 1871. The Blumlisalphorn was the first snow peak climbed (1868) by T. *with us*. My aunt was not a "grosse holländische-amerikanische Miss". She was slight and tall, while she never lived in Holland in her life, though her family came thence to New York about 1700. The ascent of the Diablerets was in 1870, not in 1872. My aunt was perfectly well in 1876 in Switzerland, and continued so until Dec. 14, 1876, when she was attacked by rheumatic fever, which went to her heart and killed her on the 19th Dec. 1876. In 1870, T. was *with us* all summer, and her son Bello was born *before* we ever saw her in 1868 for the first time. Almer was not our guide on the Diablerets, but a man from Plan des Îles. I greatly regret that you should have taken so little trouble in this matter, and would certainly not have sanctioned the appearance of the article had I seen it before publication. All the true facts as to T. are given in the 2 pamphlets I lent you, and it was quite unnecessary to invent new ones. *That* is not the right way to write history.

Little of this justified testiness appears to have clouded the young Coolidge's mind as he set out with Miss Brevoort for the first great Dauphiné campaign of 1870. Their achievements were remarkable. They met Christian Almer and his son, "young Christian"—the former being joyfully recognised by Tschingel to the pleasure of all—and together made the first ascent of the central peak of the Meije, the first ascent of the Ailefroide, and the third ascent of the Ecrins which Whymper had climbed for the first time only six years previously. They climbed the Pelvoux, then drove south by carriage across the frontier to Courmayeur, whence Coolidge made the second ascent of Mont Blanc by the Brenva route, watched with anxious eyes through a telescope by Miss Brevoort. They joined forces again, made the fifth ascent of the Dent Blanche, attempted the Weisshorn, climbed the Dom, and made a number of other less important ascents before returning to England—via the tortuous and inconvenient route necessitated by the Franco-Prussian War.

The ideal pattern of Coolidge's life had been set, and it was to be followed for the next six years during which he built up the foundation of his unique experience. Nine or ten months of the year were divided between work at Oxford—where he became a Fellow of Magdalen in 1875—visits to his aunt's establishment at Dorking, Surrey, and journeys to London where his presence in any dispute then brewing could be used to better effect. It was a satisfying and rather pleasant existence, almost insulated by scholarship and money from the outer world which at times inconveniently intruded on his ideas (". . . in that case Russia will come forward and there will be an European war, when of course my poor Dolomite plan must go to the wall", he wrote).

In 1871 Coolidge and Miss Brevoort visited the Oberland and the Pennines, Miss Brevoort losing the first lady's ascent of the Matterhorn to Lucy Walker, but gaining, as compensation, the first lady's traverse of the peak from Zermatt to Breuil. One unexpected result of the campaign was the famous paper in the *Alpine Journal* which described "A Day and a Night on the Bietschhorn", famous because although signed by Coolidge it was in fact written by Miss Brevoort, excluded by her sex from both the Alpine Club and its journal.

The following year they again went to the Oberland after only a brief visit to the Dauphiné; and, the following year, to the Dauphiné again. Early in 1874, they started the fashion for winter climbing by visiting the Oberland and making the first winter ascents of the Wetterhorn and the Jungfrau, an appetiser for yet another visit to Dauphiné later in the year. There came a visit to the Mont Blanc range in 1875 and in the following year another winter campaign in the Alps—during which three unsuccessful attempts were made to climb Mont Blanc for the first time at that season—and a three-month summer campaign that ranged along the Alps from the Dauphiné to the Dolomites.

Throughout all these expeditions in the early 1870's, the practice was for Coolidge and Miss Brevoort to make a number of climbs together, for them to separate in order to carry out any individual plans which they might have made, and to keep in touch with one another by an almost daily series of letters which criss-crossed the minor ranges and recounted the previous day's exploits. Tschingel, in general, stayed with Miss Brevoort, Coolidge, away from Miss Brevoort, generally climbed only with his guides, invariably the Almers, although it was during these years that he began his acquaintance with Arthur Fairbanks, a man of his own age, and with his lifelong friend Frederick Gardiner. He climbed with both as occasion and convenience demanded. It was obvious that he preferred the companionship of Miss Brevoort. Then in December 1876, came her sudden death.

Coolidge never quite recovered. With Meta Brevoort gone, the world would never again be quite the same place. Her death did more than create in Coolidge an abnormal affection for the Alps wherein he raised her shadow; it illuminated the way in which the mountains might carry out a dual emotional and intellectual task in the mind of a man suitably placed by circumstance. Coolidge had been inordinately fond of his aunt and with her death he was driven back on himself; simultaneously, he realised that no one had yet applied to mountains and mountaineering the technique of the historian. He had only to do so to satisfy an academic longing and, at the same time, keep alive in his mind a whole series of memories from happier days. Circumstances provided, ready-made, an intellectual field into which his emotions could be driven without too much risk of disaster.

After the death of Miss Brevoort, Coolidge's life altered; steadily he began to withdraw himself more closely into University life, and into the academic problems of Alpine history which were to be his solace for two lonely decades in Britain. In 1882 he took Holy Orders which gave effect, he said, to the wish of one whose memory was dear to him. Only two things worried him in entering the Church, he admitted. One was his dislike of having to carry out parochial work; the second was what he referred to as one circumstance in his own life which made him wish for the grace of Orders.

His interest in mountains did not diminish; it changed emphasis slightly and veered more and more towards the solution of historical problems, to the amassing of knowledge for its own sake. Coolidge continued to travel abroad each year—without Tschingel now, for during the last three years of her life she was not fit enough for the restless journeyings which he carried out. He continued to increase his already vast number of ascents, and he began to build into formidable proportions his considerable fame as an Alpine historiographer. The question of whether the original route up one particular Alpine ridge went left or right of one particular rock pinnacle would involve him for weeks in a heated and much-enjoyed argument with whomsoever was rash enough to challenge his view. He once filled pages on the question of whether or not there should be an accent over the word chalet. He had little sense of proportion, an overwhelming fear of showing his emotions, and the result was that for those beyond the small circle of Alpine enthusiasts his writings were slightly repellent with unexplained facts and figures. Even the enthusiasts were not always happy. "I personally cannot forgive him", wrote one climber, "for . . . the fact that he never tried seriously to communicate to the world the knowledge which he possessed, but was content to fling it out in a disorderly mess."

In 1880 he became editor of the *Alpine Journal* in succession to Douglas Freshfield, a post which brought him into touch, and frequently into conflict, with the leading mountaineers of the period. His fame was already such that not only experienced mountaineers but also embryonic climbers, topographers, map-makers, the newspapers, and even dear old souls who wanted a quiet holiday in Switzerland, wrote to Coolidge for advice. They invariably got it, courteously, *in extenso*, and—most annoying thing of all for his enemies—correctly.

Only when Coolidge's accuracy was questioned, when his opinions were challenged, or when he imagined that he was the butt of some sly joke that he scarcely comprehended, only then did he really rise in his anger and show, as one critic expressed it, that "in his one-sidedness, savagery, and bitterness he was medieval".

He was easy to cross, and somewhat feared, as is shown by the small illustration which appears in the volume of the Badminton library that deals with mountaineering. This shows railway porters manhandling the baggage and impedimenta of what is obviously a group of climbing friends on their way to the Alps. The original sketch was drawn by that austere autocrat, Sir Edward Davidson, Coolidge's opponent in one of the most bitter of Alpine controversies; on the luggage Davidson inscribed the initials C. T. D. (Clinton Dent), D. W. F. (Douglas Freshfield), W. M. C. (William Martin Conway), and, A. J. B. (A. J. Butler, another of Coolidge's opponents, about whom he wrote virulent, not to say scurrilous, letters); and, flying from the parrot cage perched on A. J. B.'s luggage, he put a tag with the initials W. A. B. C. At the special request of the editor, who feared a libel suit, the initials were finally altered to A. B. C. Coolidge had already justified the writer of *The Times'* obituary who described him as an adept in the gentle art of making enemies and a man who regarded a hatchet as an instrument not for burying but for use.

Coolidge had always suffered from bad health. He had no particular love of either Britain or the British mountains—he had no interest either in the British hills, to which the Pilkingtons tried to entice him, or in the Himalayas—and in 1896 he moved from Oxford to Grindelwald, first taking up residence with the Almers and then renting his own house, the Chalet Montana, in the village. Here, among his Alpine library of some 15,000 volumes, he became a legend; from "the fiery lamb" he was gradually transformed into "the sage of Grindelwald". It was here that his best and most scholarly work was done.

Earlier, he had revised Murray's *Switzerland*; he had become the Alpine contributor to the *Encyclopaedia Britannica*, contributing more than 200 articles to one edition of the work, and of half a dozen other popular encyclopaediae. He had produced *Swiss Travel and Swiss Guide-Books*, an erudite, unreadable, volume in which Leslie Stephen found "a great deal of interesting matter".

> You have, I think [Stephen continued in a letter to Coolidge] conclusively proved one point viz. that you should write a "special" guidebook, the speciality in your case being history. Even in my scrambles, I used often to think that a book enabling one to look on a few historical associations to Alpine sites would greatly add to the pleasure; and I am sure that if done with discretion i.e. not making too severe demands upon the general reader, a most charming book might be put together. You could do it admirably, though I admit that the task would not be a light one.

Coolidge glossed over the charm, but before his move to Grindelwald he had contributed many of the 220 items in the bibliography of his writings which he later had privately printed.

At Grindelwald, less disturbed by friends and acquaintances, he produced his major works. The first was a new edition of Ball's *Guide to the Western Alps*, a publication over which he had quarrelled with the Alpine Club for years. There were arguments about how the revision of Ball—which by the 1890's was seriously out of date—should be handled; about who the helpers should be, and on the amount of editorial authority that Coolidge should have over them. There were, after all, many precedents for similar disputes—Coolidge had resigned from his post as editor of Murray when John Murray refused to print Coolidge's libellous note on an Alpine hotel. Coolidge had taken on Ball in 1893 but illness, and his residence abroad, conspired to delay publication of the volume until 1898. The next year he resigned from the Alpine Club after a dispute over the second volume of the work.

Although Coolidge was to be made an honorary member of the Club in 1904—an honorary membership which he resigned six years later following yet another dispute—the break of 1899 somehow underlined his divorce from Britain and his thirty-year residence there. Alpine history had become more than the passion of his life; it had become life itself.

Cared for by Albert his manservant, rarely going into the village of Grindelwald—yet succeeding in quarrelling with "young" Christian Almer, and somehow knowing most of the village gossip—Coolidge worked with and for his library of books that overflowed into the corridors and rooms of his house. With their help he produced, in 1904, the monumental *Josias Simler et les Origines de l'Alpinisme jusqu'où 1600*, a book whose character can be gathered from the fact that it contained 190 pages of introduction, 307 of text, 130 of notes, 327 of appendices, 62 of notes on the appendices, and a 29-page index. Four years later there came *The Alps in Nature and History*, a volume in which Coolidge for the first time began to interpolate some

30 A Group taken in the late 1860's showing (*right couple*) Miss Straton and Jean Charlet, the Guide whom she later married

… at the Grands Mulets, Mont Blanc, in 1864, at the age of 14

of his own reminiscences, a practice he expanded in *Alpine Studies* four years later. In every other way Coolidge remained the same unemotional recording-machine of facts, dates, and figures.

When war broke out in 1914 he applied for a British passport since he no longer qualified for U.S. citizenship. The British refused, on the grounds that he had not spent the previous few years in Britain and therefore lacked a residence qualification. Coolidge argued; he had, he pointed out, sworn allegiance to the Queen once when he became a Fellow of Magdalen and yet again when he took Holy Orders. He still failed to get his passport, and became both "the man without a country" and "the first displaced person".

During the latter years of the war he began editing the vast diaries of his old friend, Tuckett, and these were finally published, in 1920, as *A Pioneer in the High Alps*. Coolidge was by this time thinking of the future; what worried him most was the fate of the great library which he had built up over the years. In 1907 he had offered the Alpine portion of it to the Alpine Club; the President, in thanking him for the offer, had not unnaturally suggested that the offer should be put in legal form. Coolidge, leaping at the chance of taking umbrage, replied furiously and suggested that the offer had been turned down. Now, in the early 1920's, he was thinking again.

First, he considered giving at least a portion of it to the John Rylands Library in Manchester, and in a letter to a friend discussing the matter he described the collection, which was insured for £3,000.

> I hope that if you ever come to this place [Grindelwald], you will look in on me, and examine my library of 16,000 volumes, particularly the Alpine and the Swiss History portions. It represents the accumulations of 50 years, for I am now 71½ years of age. It fills 12 rooms of the rather large wooden house which I inhabit, and its disposal has given me a good deal of trouble, as I wished certain portions of it to be kept together, if possible. I first offered the Alpine portion, with various Alpine curiosities, to the Alpine Club of London—as a free legacy. I was much surprised when this

offer was refused, on the strange ground that I could give certain books, but not a whole section of the library. So I had to look around. The Bodleian desired to *purchase* the Alpine and Swiss history portions, but insisted on an *immediate* purchase (this was before the war), to which I could not consent, as I did not feel that my literary activity was yet ended and required that it should be valued by an English expert, to which I could not consent for I do not think any English expert is capable of valuing, at any rate, the Swiss history portion. So I fell back, as to the Alpine portion, on a very old and intimate Liverpool friend, rather older than I was—but unluckily he died in 1919!

Finally, the library was bequeathed to the Swiss Alpine Club. Coolidge died in 1926. Almost until the end he was still sending out his famous yellow postcards, either badly typed or inscribed in a small spidery writing with pertinent comments on some Alpine controversy. Almost until the end he was visited by old Alpine friends from Britain who would call and be received by him, and then be shown round his library. For the people of Grindelwald—who to this day care for his grave in Grindelwald churchyard—he had a curiosity value; he belonged to the past that had existed before the cult of mountains had begun.

> His great knowledge, expended without stint for the benefit of mountaineers of the world, gave him such a claim to universal recognition that any foibles were willingly accepted [said one mountaineer who had crossed swords with him more than once]. But for his great labours he would have no doubt been considered a quarrelsome old devil.

More of his friends would have been present at the funeral had it not been for the General Strike. As it was, the whole of Grindelwald turned out, men, women, and children standing in the keen air of the lovely spring day or following the cortège as it wound from the Chalet Montana, at the southern end of the village, past the English church where Coolidge had preached more than once, up the gentle rise to the little church beneath the shadow of the Wetterhorn.

The sun shone brilliantly, occasionally loosening the winter snow still lying on the heights. As the coffin was lowered into the grave there came the distant rumble of an avalanche, pouring off the cliffs of the Eiger, a last tribute from the mountains at whose significance Coolidge might openly have scoffed but which he would have privately considered no more than his due.

Chapter Eight

THE WOMEN

With head on high she trod,
A youthful, seeking, maid,
With eyes alight for distant height
Unawed and unafraid.
How can we seek an equal peak
Where we can walk with God?

ANON.

MISS BREVOORT, whose attraction to mountain-climbing had so influenced Coolidge's whole life, was one of the first women to make any number of serious high Alpine climbs. She followed the example of Lucy Walker, another remarkable woman who was the daughter of one enthusiastic Liverpool climber and the sister of another; between them Miss Brevoort and Miss Walker account for most of the important climbs made by women during the 1860's.

Before their day, two women had climbed Mont Blanc—Maria Paradis in 1809 and Henriette d'Angeville in 1838—but both ascents were exceptional events, the first being made for profit and the second for the notoriety which it gave.

Maria, an eighteen-year-old peasant girl who owned a small stall near the foot of the mountain, did not enjoy the ascent. "Throw me into a crevasse and go on yourselves", she implored her guides. They humanely ignored her request, dragged her to the top, where she arrived in poor condition, and brought her safely back to Chamonix.

Henriette d'Angeville, the "thwarted maiden lady in her forties" as she has been called, was of different metal. "She goes as well as we do and fears nothing", said one of her guides, all of whom were so impressed with her performance that on reaching the summit they lifted her on their shoulders, saying as they did so: "Now, Mademoiselle, you shall go one higher than Mont Blanc." Being a staunch Royalist, she drank a bumper of champagne to the Comte de Paris, and then despatched a carrier pigeon with the news of her success. Her dress, in which she was later painted, consisted of a long-skirted garment which she wore over brightly checkered peg-top trousers, an outfit chosen, one must assume, for its publicity value rather than its utility.

Throughout the 1840's and 1850's, a number of women began to travel through the less-known parts of the Alps even though they did not make any major ascents. The wives of George Barnard and Michael Faraday went with their husbands on a leisurely tour of the Oberland in 1841. In the following decade the wives of Gilbert and Churchill accompanied the party which made pioneering journeys through the Dolomites. Mrs. Freshfield, mother of Douglas Freshfield, and Mrs. Cole, both travelled around and across the Alps during the 1850's, and Mrs. Wills was taken for a night on the Mer de Glace while on her honeymoon. There were also the two unknown ladies "past the noon of life", whom Mrs. Cole met in Aosta after they had just crossed the Mont Blanc range with a single guide.

Two things combined to hinder the growth of mountain-climbing among women. One was the belief that it was not a womanly occupation, a belief which was expressed until well past the turn of the century. The second was the problem of clothes.

The male attitude was well described by Ellen Pigeon, one of two famous sisters who in 1869 made the first crossing of the Sesiajoch into Italy and took charge of the party when their solitary guide lost the way.

> In days gone by [she wrote to Coolidge in 1892] many A.C.'s would not speak to us, though no one was so impertinent as "the king of the Riffel". Now, people are accustomed to lady climbers, and even solitary ones. We were the first, I think, to go unattended by a male protector, and we got on very well, but then two together must be pleasanter than one alone, when you must have guides.

"The king of the Riffel" was Sir W. E. Davidson, Permanent Legal Adviser to the Foreign Office for more than thirty years, who between 1875 and his retirement from active mountaineering nearly forty years later, climbed the Riffelhorn above Zermatt 250 times. Aloof, distinguished, highly critical of innovation, he held opinions on the propriety of women on the mountains that may well be imagined even though they have nowhere been recorded.

Even as late as 1879, the feeling against women climbers was strong, and Mrs. Aubrey le Blond, the remarkable thrice-married woman who was the founder of the first woman's climbing club in Britain, met considerable opposition.

> I had to struggle hard for my freedom [she says]. My mother faced the music on my behalf when my grand aunt, Lady Bentinck, sent out a frantic S.O.S.—"Stop her climbing mountains. She is scandalising all London and looks like a Red Indian."

The second thing which hampered the development of climbing among women was the question of dress. Some of the first advice came from Mrs. Cole.

> Every lady engaged on an Alpine journey should have a dress of some light woollen material, such as carmelite or alpaca which, in the case of bad weather, does not look utterly forlorn when it has once been wetted and dried [she advised].
>
> Small rings should be sewn inside the seam of the dress, and a cord passed through them, the ends of which should be knotted together in such a way that the whole dress may be drawn up at a moment's notice, to the required height. A riding skirt, without a body, which can be slipped off and on in a moment, is also invaluable.

The "slipping on and off" school grew throughout the years. A skirt was invariably considered necessary for appearances when leaving or arriving at an Alpine inn or hotel; breeches or their equivalent were essential to the conquest of certain mountain obstacles, and to the safe traverse of more than one narrow ridge. The discardable skirt theory could bring its own penalties, however, and it was Mrs. Aubrey le Blond, when traversing the Zinal Rothhorn, who remembered on approaching Zinal that she had left her skirt on the far side of the mountain, and was forced to retrace most of her day's route.

Miss Brevoort, who on at least one occasion was driven to the use of trousers, was perpetually experimenting, and records that: "My dress plan, too, has failed, and descending snow slopes the snow enters the rings and stuffs up the hem and makes me heavy and wet. I have had to baste up both dress and skirt."

Yet Meta Brevoort's model, Miss Lucy Walker, never used the subterfuge of men's clothes, wearing on the mountains a white print dress whose shape she carefully had "renewed" whenever an expedition was finished.

In the self-assured way in which she made her early ascents, Lucy Walker was typical of the new race of women which the Victorian Age produced. She "aspired" to the mountains; she felt drawn to them by an inexpressible attraction whose rightness, had it ever been in doubt, would have been assured by the fact that her father and brother were ardent devotees of the sport. Lucy Walker *knew* that climbing was *better* than the other occupations in which ladies could indulge. It brought her into contact with nature; it gave her the illusion of danger which had almost been removed from the world in which she moved; it gave her contacts with a world of people different from those she normally knew. It brought her, with its combination of excitement, beauty, and exaltation, to the edge of a new world.

Her first glimpse of that world came in 1859. Lucy Walker was twenty-eight at the time, a spectacled, darkly ringletted young woman, amply fashioned and kindly. She had arrived at the Schwarenbach Inn with her family, wished to make the ascent of the Altels, and was told by her father that Melchior Anderegg was the best guide for the expedition. Outside the inn, she asked a young man, apparently a porter, where she could find the famous guide. Drawing himself up to his full height, he replied with dignity, "I am Anderegg." It was the beginning of a long and increasingly friendly association. During the following twenty-one years, Lucy Walker made ninety-eight expeditions, only three of them unsuccessfully, mostly in the company of her brother, her father, or Melchior Anderegg. In all of these adventures she consistently refused to dress like a man, maintaining with perfect reason that she preferred to travel thus even if it did slightly limit her climbing.

Her views were strong, and she was always pleased to explain why she had not climbed one particular summit. "You said that no woman could manage it", a certain woman climber had said to a well-known mountaineer after her ascent of the peak. "No", he replied, "I said, 'No lady'."

On the mountains she took nothing to eat except sponge-cake and champagne—or sometimes *asti*—both wines which she found ideal in combating the slight mountain-sickness from which she suffered throughout the whole of her climbing career. She did not ride, fish, or even walk with any particular enthusiasm, her only outdoor exercise other than climbing being the gentle one of croquet.

Among the few women who climbed during the same years as did Lucy Walker, were Emmeline Lewis-Lloyd and Miss Straton, a remarkable couple who invariably travelled on the mountains together. Miss Lloyd, brought up at Nantgwyllt in mid-Wales, a great house which was swamped when the Elan Dam was built to create the water-supply for Birmingham, was a famous local sportswoman. Short, stout, and jovial, she enjoyed the reputation of once having played a salmon from sunrise to sundown, after which the local population came to regale her in the battle, with drink and sandwiches.

She enters into early mountaineering quite confident and self-assured, and appears rarely to have been surprised at any turn which events might take. One evening she was completing a solitary scramble in the snow above Gressoney when there appeared in the distance a figure which seemed to be that of a local chamois-hunter. He came up to her, bowed, and began to talk with her in perfect English; discussing the mountains, he escorted her back to her hotel where he was apparently known to the staff. After he had left, Miss Lloyd casually asked his name. "King Victor-Emmanuel", she was told.

Until 1873, Miss Lewis-Lloyd's most constant companion on the mountains was a character remarkable at any time, a spinster

32 Queen Victoria ascending Lochnagar, near Balmoral, in the early 1850's
From the painting by Carl Haag, 1853

Two Of The Later Victorian Women Climbers

33 Mrs. Jackson

34
Miss Maud Meyer

endowed with £4,000 a year who married her Alpine guide and lived happily with him for the rest of her life. Miss Straton, who achieved the remarkable feat, first visited the Alps in 1861 at the age of twenty-three, but it was not until four years later that she began a long series of Alpine excursions, many of them in the company of Jean Charlet of Chamonix. She appears to have met him first at Nantgwyllt, where he had been brought by Miss Lloyd to work as a groom for a year. She travelled with him in the Pyrenees, then in the Alps—where she made four ascents of Mont Blanc—married him and settled happily in a small home near Chamonix where she spent the rest of her life. Of their two sons, one was later to climb Mont Blanc at the age of thirteen, the other at the age of eleven and a half. Neither, Miss Straton later proudly recorded, needed special help.

Both Miss Straton and Miss Lewis-Lloyd appear to have been attracted to mountaineering largely because they felt it wrong that any pastime should be reserved for the male sex alone. They tackled the situation with energy, courage, determination, and the banner of emancipation flying high. It seems unlikely that they were moved by the mountains in quite the same way as Lucy Walker and Meta Brevoort, although they had attempted the Matterhorn as early as 1869.

Miss Brevoort, whose Alpine story is so closely linked with that of Coolidge, was brought up in a Paris convent school. She was neither strong nor unwomanly, and she appears to have had a flair for figuring in colourful and rather startling incidents. Early in her Alpine career she climbed Mont Blanc with two guides and Madame Sylvain-Couttet, the wife of one of them. Then the party drank the customary bumper of champagne, following which the four danced a quadrille in the bright sun and sang the "Marseillaise", a banned song in those days of the Second Empire.

She was a woman of immense vitality, and a typical picture of her is given by John Stogdon, a mountaineer who gave up plans for Himalayan exploring when he married. Coolidge was studying at the Bel Alp and Miss Brevoort was invited to join a party that included Stogdon and the Rev. Arthur Fairbanks.

Her courage and exuberant enjoyment doubled our pleasure [he recalled years later]. She was ready for anything. One crevasse, of which we could see no end, was too broad for her to jump, but she jumped at my rash proposal that we should let her down into it till she could find a ledge to stand on. We paid her out some forty feet, but I thought we should never have got her up again. You can't get a direct pull. However, in spite of cut knuckles, she thoroughly enjoyed it.

It was a tragedy of Miss Brevoort's life that her two greatest Alpine ambitions were both frustrated. One of these was to be the first woman to ascend the Matterhorn, a feat for which she had everything ready in 1871, having unsuccessfully attempted the mountain from the Italian side in 1869. One of her guides incautiously mentioned the plans to Melchior Anderegg who immediately hurried off to Zermatt, as loyalty bade him, where he knew that the Walkers could be found. Plans were quickly formed, and on July 21 he led Lucy Walker, Francis Walker, her father, and Frederick Gardiner, to the summit. Miss Brevoort, arriving in Zermatt a few days later, was greeted with the news that "the young lady has just come down from the Matterhorn". Both women had nearly been preceded by Felicité Carrel, daughter of an Italian guide—not the great Carrel—who four years earlier had reached to within 350 ft. of the summit with a party which climbed the Italian ridge.

Miss Brevoort, who a few days after the Walkers' ascent made the first woman's traverse of the mountain by ascending from Zermatt and descending the southern side into Italy, had one ambition even stronger than that of making the first woman's ascent of the Matterhorn. She desired, possibly more than anything else on earth, to be the first woman on top of the Meije in the Dauphiné. Together with Coolidge, she had made the first ascent of one of the lower peaks in 1870; and, with him, had gone back year after year, her hopes continually deferred by bad weather.

In 1876 there came the chance of attempting the peak for which she had mortgaged considerable emotional energy. She gave it up so that Coolidge should have more money for climbing in the Dauphiné while she, her eyes on the expenses, remained carefully in the Oberland. There was news that others had their eyes on the Meije, then still unclimbed by either man or woman; Miss Brevoort's letter to Coolidge from the Oberland came straight from the heart.

> Alas, to think of all the others who will be coming, and of the *one* who may succeed [she wrote]. Give my love to all my dear old friends now in your sight and specially to that glorious Meije and ask her to keep herself for me.

Within a few months of having written the letter, Miss Brevoort was dead. Her nephew, hoping to make the first ascent in her name, was preceded in 1877 by Boileau de Castelnau, a young Frenchman. Coolidge made the second ascent the following year, but it was not until 1888 that Kathleen Richardson, the legendary Miss Richardson as the French called her, was to make the first ascent of the peak by a lady.

Miss Richardson was the antithesis of the typical woman climber of the period. Slender, short, looking rather like a piece of carefully kept Dresden china, she was the most remarkable of the women mountaineers who immediately followed Miss Brevoort's generation. Brown-haired, green-eyed, frail-looking, she was, in fact, tough and indefatigable. "She does not eat, and she walks like a devil", the guides said of her.

She was on the Hornli at the age of sixteen and a few months after her seventeenth birthday carried out her first campaign in the Engadine, where she climbed the Piz Languard and the Piz Corvatsch.

During the following eleven seasons she completed 116 *grandes courses* and sixty minor ascents, six of them being first ascents by any mountaineer, another fourteen of them first ascents by a woman.

The most remarkable of the first was her ascent of the Aiguille de Bionnassay and the traverse of the East arête, a route often attempted and considered impossible. Later in the same season she heard that an Englishwoman whose name no one knew was about to make the first ascent on the Meije. She hurried south to the Dauphiné, only to find that the Englishwoman was herself. She justified the rumour that had gone before her, climbing the mountain in a single day from La Bérarde.

Many of Miss Richardson's climbs were made with Mlle Mary Paillon, the famous French Alpinist who nearly killed her companion on the Central Aiguille d'Arves when the Frenchwoman's skirts dislodged a stone which crashed down on Miss Richardson's head. When the couple were within a few yards of the summit, Miss Richardson, having changed places with her friend, waited for Mlle Paillon to reach her, then pushed her ahead with the words. "You go first. I have the Meije. You take the Aiguille d'Arves."

By Miss Richardson's day, women climbers had become increasingly numerous. One of the most remarkable among them was the woman who is most generally remembered as Mrs. Aubrey le Blond.

Born of a wealthy Irish family, she first visited Switzerland because of her poor health, was attracted by the mountains, made the ascent of Mont Blanc almost by accident, and showed her attitude when she later wrote that she owed "a supreme debt of gratitude to the mountains for knocking from me the shackles of conventionality".

For years she thought it only right that she should travel in the mountains with her ladies' maid. Only when one had eloped with a courier and another developed hysteria whenever her mistress was late in returning from a climb, did she dispense with such women.

Her importance was that she took it for granted that women should climb, and should do so on equal terms with men. When Roman Imboden, the son of her favourite guide, and a man with whom she had frequently climbed, was killed in the Alps, she felt compelled to give up mountaineering in the Alps; habit was too much, however, and for season after season she visited Norway, making there a series of first ascents almost comparable to that of Cecil Slingsby.

Like Maud Meyer, Maths Tutor at Girton and a later President of the Ladies' Alpine Club which Mrs. Le Blond helped to found, she represented the last struggle of the Victorian woman climber freeing herself from the prejudice of the past; like Maud Meyer, her remarkable record carried on not only into the Edwardian but into the Georgian era.

Both women are symbols of the triumph achieved when women on the mountains were first judged equally with men—Miss Meyer met, and was apparently unrebuked by, Sir W. E. Davidson who had so criticised the Pigeons. Both women showed by the multiplicity of their interests, by their courage, and by their devoted interest in mountains through years of hard work, a reflection of the earlier Victorian male mountaineers whom they resemble so much.

Mrs. Le Blond did not die until 1934, leaving behind her a memory of tremendous accomplishments and more than half a dozen books in which she exhorted her fellows up into the mountains.

Miss Meyer, whose record included more than a hundred expeditions—each of them neatly recorded in an edition of Coolidge's *Alps in Nature and History*—continued climbing high mountains until eighteen months before her death at the age of sixty-one.

Her death was in keeping.

> For some years she had been bicycling all over London to her various mathematical coaching appointments [says a surviving relative]. Everybody warned her of the dangers of this procedure, at her age, and in London's growing traffic. She replied that she liked it, that it kept her fit, and there was a spice of excitement about it; if she got killed, it was entirely her responsibility, and you might as well die that way as any other.

She did.

Chapter Nine

THE MOUNTAINEERS IN BRITAIN

For me this land, that sea, these airs, those folk and fields suffice.
What purple Southern pomp can match our changeful Northern skies,
Black with December snows unshed or pearled with August haze—
The clanging arch of steel-grey March, or June's long-lighted days?

KIPLING

IT was in the 1880's that the activities of Cecil Slingsby and of a small handful of other enthusiasts began to form the *corpus* of knowledge and tradition around which climbing in Britain was to grow.

Men had, of course, found pleasure on the British hills before the Victorian Alpinists devoted themselves to the matter. The Highland Mountain Club of Lochgoilhead, which held its annual meetings on Midsummer Day to climb a local hill and to carry on there "certain festivities", was founded in 1815. The Gaiter Club, which in 1911 offered financial help to the Scottish Mountaineering Club for the publication of its guide-books, had been founded by the then Lord Inverclyde in 1849. The Cobbler Club, the first club in Britain whose main purpose was the encouragement of mountain-climbing, was founded in Glasgow in 1866 for those who wanted "to climb the Cobbler and whatever other worthy hill can be reached in the course of a Saturday expedition from Glasgow". The Perthshire Mountain Club, started in 1875 as a section of the Perthshire Society of Natural History, initiated its members with due ceremony at the top of a 3,000-footer whose ascent was the qualification for entry, and utilised the services of a cairn-master and of a bard who recited a specially written poem.

South of the Border, there came Mathews' "Society of Welsh

Rabbits" and, later, the Yorkshire Ramblers' Club in whose formation Cecil Slingsby played such a prominent part. All these clubs, and the others which sprang up in the 1890's, were the crystallisation of a process which had begun in the middle of the century, when the enthusiasm of the earlier Alpine climbers, taking a casual week-end in North Wales or the Lakes, had begun to act upon the local fell-walkers.

The Queen herself was not without influence. A poor view is generally taken of her reaction to mountain-climbing, but it is not true that after the Matterhorn accident she attempted to have climbing forbidden; she merely made a note of the fact in her diary—"four poor Englishmen including a brother of Lord Queensberry have lost their lives in Switzerland, descending over a dangerous place from the Matterhorn and falling over a precipice". It was only after three serious accidents in the summer of 1882 that she made any move.

Then on August 24, 1882, Sir Henry Ponsonby, her private secretary, wrote to Mr. Gladstone.

> The Queen [he said] commands me to ask you if you think she can say anything to mark her disapproval of the dangerous Alpine excursions which this year have occasioned so much loss of life.

Gladstone, who appears to have been on the side of the angels, suggested that no action be taken.

> I do not wonder [he said] that the Queen's sympathetic feelings have again been excited by the accidents, so grave in character, and so accumulated during recent weeks, on the Alps. But I doubt the possibility of any interference, even by her Majesty, with a prospect of advantage. It may be questionable whether, upon the whole, mountain-climbing (and be it remembered that Snowdon has its victims as well as the Matterhorn) is more destructive than various other pursuits in the way of recreation which perhaps have no justification to plead so respectable as that which may be alleged on behalf of mountain expeditions. The question, however, is not one of wisdom or unwisdom; but viewing it, as you put it, upon its very definite and simple grounds, I see no room for action.

Yet these comments were not made known at the time. For the mass of mankind, the Queen was the monarch who had commanded a special performance of Albert Smith's "Mont Blanc", who had fallen in love with the Cairngorms, had ascended Lochnagar and many other peaks surrounding Balmoral—on pony, it is true—and had later shown by her *Leaves from A Journal of Our Life in the Highlands* that she had a genuine delight in the glories of the mountains. She allowed Prince Arthur, Duke of Connaught, to reach the Grands Mulets on Mont Blanc in 1864, even though she did not allow him to continue to the summit and become the youngest person—he was then 14—who had attained it. Little of this was "mountaineering", yet it did make more understandable in the public mind the growing association between the "Alpinists" and the local fell-walkers.

Many of these fell-walkers and hill-wanderers were formidable men. There was, for instance, that queer unidentified figure after whom was named the Parson's Nose, the fine rock-snout that thrusts itself out into Cwm Glas.

This clergyman described by John Henry Cliffe was, he says,

> possessed of a most extraordinary mania for climbing mountains. Picture to yourself a tall man, about 52 years of age, of a wiry, spare habit, rather slightly built, dressed in a pair of dingy slop trousers, a linen spencer of the same complexion, without hat or covering of any sort for the head, no neck-tie, his shirt-collar unbuttoned, with an enormous alpenstock or climbing pole, seven or eight feet in length, in his hand, and you may perhaps be able to form some idea of the strange grotesque figure we have endeavoured to describe. His object was, to use his own expression, "to follow the skyline", until he reached the summit; he would then descend the other side of the mountain towards Beddgelert, in a similar manner. He most frequently performed his excursions alone, although occasionally, when not so familiar with the locality, he availed himself of the services of a guide. He would follow up these rambles *de die in diem*, regardless of the weather, and was generally on his legs from about nine a.m. until eight p.m. The most extraordinary thing was, how he could keep up such violent daily exercise without any refreshment

35 Cecil Slingsby, in 1876, at the age of 27

whatever during the period he was among the mountains. To prevent thirst, he carried a small pebble in his mouth; and Harry Owen, the guide, assured us that he never saw him partake of anything to eat or drink, not even a cup of cold water, while on an excursion. We have several times met him on his return to the inn (Pen-y-Gwryd), drenched with perspiration, and whilst his dinner was being prepared, he would continue at gentle exercise (staff in hand), to "cool down"—like a race-horse after a "breather"—preparatory to partaking of his repast—in fine weather generally *al fresco*—exhibiting not the least apparent fatigue. He was a man of very temperate habits; two or three glasses of sherry were the extent of his libations; he avoided smoking and he would be up early in the morning performing his ablutions for several hours. He appeared to have no other object in climbing to the wild mountain-tops than merely (as he said) to behold the wonderful works of the Almighty.

What the climbing parson was to Wales, Frederick Bowring was to the Lakes. Both men broke away from the tradition of making only certain set and "popular" ascents—although Bowring climbed Great Gable more than a hundred times—and both provided a nucleus of non-professional local knowledge on which the Alpine Club men of the sixties and seventies could draw.

Bowring, who was born in 1823 and did not die until 1918, must have been as striking a figure as the climbing parson. And, like him, Bowring climbed and walked with great vigour and precision when he was nearing the age of sixty.

His long legs were clad in thick trousers; his fine head (which strikingly resembled that of the poet Tennyson) was covered with a felt hat, the wide brim of which had been reduced to limpness by his habit of securing it in windy weather by means of an immense blue kerchief tied under his chin. The "Norfolk" jacket was too modern for him and his usual coat bore somewhat bunchy tails with huge pockets which contained, as a minimum, maps, compass, string, field-glasses, sandwiches, and the afore-mentioned blue bandana, gloves, a large grey woollen comforter, and several books, besides abundant materials for smoking. In his hand was a stout six-foot fell-pole with a forked spike, which he thought less liable to slip on rocks.

The third, and possibly the most eccentric of all these early fell-walkers was the Rev. James Jackson. A tall, bearded character who had served with the British forces during the early Napoleonic wars and then, relinquishing this career for the Church, he had served in a variety of incumbencies throughout the North of England, and astounded his congregations almost as much by his egotistical verses as by his prodigious feats of walking.

In his sixty-ninth year, he walked forty-six miles in fourteen and a half hours, followed this up two days later with fifty-six miles in eighteen hours, and, after another two days, with sixty miles in less than twenty hours.

His character is best shown by the incident of the weather-cock on his church steeple at Rivington. When steeplejacks refused to go up to it to carry out a repair, Jackson himself swarmed up the spire and commemorated the incident with a ditty which went:

Who has not heard of Steeple Jack
That lion-hearted Saxon?
Though I'm not he, he was my sire
For I am Steeple Jackson!

He became one of the most persistent fell-ramblers and -scramblers, although for years he believed that the Pillar was inaccessible. Then he read an account in a local paper of how the Westmorland brothers and their sister Kate had climbed to the top. This was too much for Steeple Jackson, even though he was then seventy-nine. Thus, on May 31, 1875, he clambered to the top alone, carrying a rope and wearing nailed shoes. Arrived on the summit, he deposited the religious relics he had brought home from Loretto—a Victorian version of the contemporary crosses on Alpine peaks—and recorded his ascent in a Greek inscription which he proudly described as "written without specs". He immediately dubbed himself the "Patriarch of the Pillarites", nominated a friend as "Patriarch Presumptive", and commemorated the event thus:

If this in your mind you will fix
When I make the Pillar my toy,
I was born in 1, 7, 9, 6,
And you'll think me a nimble old boy.

When he was eighty-two, he set out with the intention of making his second ascent of the Pillar; after two days' absence, he was found in Great Doup, the hollow near by, having apparently mistaken his position in the mist and plunged 300 ft. to his death. On a piece of paper in his pocket, carefully wrapped and put into a bottle which he had planned to leave on the summit, were his last lines:

Two elephantine properties are mine
For I can bend to pick up pin or plack:
And when this year the Pillar Rock I climb
Four score and two's the howdah on my back.

Judged by modern standards, Jackson was merely a rather incautious scrambler. Yet it was just such men who helped to acquire the considerable body of knowledge which was available by the 1880's; knowledge used by those men with experience of the Alps who during ruminating strolls on the hills cast enquiring glances at the gullies which might, in heavy snow, provide them with a few hundred feet of sport.

Charles Packe, that pioneer of the Pyrenees and the author of a guide to the range that is still so readable, was scrambling about the Lakeland fells—invariably with his Pyrenean mountain dogs—as early as 1850 and a few years later was camping and sleeping-out on them in his home-designed sleeping-bags. In the late 1850's, he introduced John Ball, Hinchliff, and William Longman to both the Lakeland fells and the hills of North Wales, and his rambling and scrambling tours continued for fifty years until within a few years of his death at the age of seventy.

Leslie Stephen, the Rev. Julius Elliott, who made the second ascent of the Matterhorn from Zermatt before being killed on the Schreckhorn by an unwary and unroped jump, and C. A. O. Baumgartner, are only three of the many climbers from the Alps who made early ascents of the Pillar Rock. Stephen climbed wherever and whenever he could, and there is at least one record of him, gangling and prehensile, ascending a chimney near Gurnard's Head, on those granite cliff-faces to which the Climbers' Club have recently issued a new guide-book.

In Scotland it was such men as Horace Walker, veteran of the famous first ascent of the Brenva Ridge of Mont Blanc, the Pilkingtons, Norman Collie, Slingsby, and Solly, all of them famous Alpine climbers, who were to make so many of the pioneer ascents in Skye and on Ben Nevis.

In Wales, one finds Professor Tyndall, Macdonald, Moore, Grove, and Tuckett among the regular week-enders. In 1879 an Alpine Club meeting was held at Capel Curig, in North Wales, while the following year no less than twenty Alpine Club members accompanied by one of the most famous lady mountaineers of the time, made the first ascent of Cust's Gully on Great End in the Lakes.

These enthusiasts from the Alps who gradually took over from the "local men" found, as the Badminton volume on "Mountaineering" later put it, that "the British hills afford endless opportunities for the gratification of our climbing instincts and for the cultivation of all those faculties, habits, and virtues, which collectively form the art of mountaineering".

The revelation came slowly, over a period of years, and would have come more slowly still had it not been for an article which Professor Tyndall contributed to the *Saturday Review* in 1861.

> Tainted by the city air [he wrote] and with gases not natural to the atmosphere of London, I gladly chimed in with the proposal of an experienced friend to live four clear days at Christmas on Welsh mutton and mountain air.

He arrived at Bethesda with Professor Huxley and Mr. Busk, and after the party had bought rake-handles at fourpence each and had converted them into alpenstocks, they finally reached Capel Curig. The following morning they set out for Snowdon, three middle-aged gentlemen, tramping through the thick snow on what must have appeared in those days a rather crazy Christmas adventure.

Tyndall was at this time an experienced mountaineer. Not only had he ascended Mont Blanc three times, but he had reached 13,000 ft. on the Matterhorn (the highest point then gained) and had earned a reputation among the Alpine fraternity for a daring that hardly matched the slow-dying view—sternly supported by Tyndall himself—that men climbed mountains merely to carry out scientific observations.

Yet the man's enthusiasm was kindled by the Welsh hills just as it had been in the Alps. On the summit of Snowdon, the view he said, "would bear comparison with the splendours of the Alps themselves". Here was enthusiasm for the British hills which would have sounded extravagant from any climber of those days, let alone from the dispassionate Tyndall. The result, not so much of this article itself, but of the interest which it aroused, was a steady growth of climbing, in England, Scotland, and Wales, by men from the Alps who even a few years earlier would have scorned the suggestion that Britain contained anything comparable to the Alps.

From the 1880's onwards, there was apparent a subtle but significant change in the records, interests, and ideals of the men to be found climbing in Britain.

There were some, such as Slingsby or Hastings or Solly, who appeared to devote almost as much time and attention to the Lakes, to Wales, or to Scotland, as they did to the mountains abroad. There was an increasing influx of young men, such as Haskett-Smith, who climbed in Britain for a number of seasons before visiting the Alps at all. And there finally developed such climbers as Archer-Thomson and O. G. Jones who went abroad only rarely and whose main interest was concentrated on the climbing, mainly rock-climbing as opposed to snow- and ice-work, which was to be found on the British crags.

Simultaneously, there is to be sensed a change of emphasis in the reasons for which most men went mountaineering. As climbing in Britain became more surely divorced from climbing in the Alps during the last quarter of the century, so did the basic reasons which drove men up into the hills become more divorced from the weighty problems that had troubled the thinkers of a decade or so earlier. Trevelyan's comment that "all the thought of the age arose out of the circumstances of the age" is no less true of the second than it was of the first half of the Victorian era. And, by the 1880's, matters both temporal and spiritual were far easier than they had been two decades earlier. There might still be worries about the problems posed by the scientists, but the first awful impact of Darwin had passed, and the Church had, as it were, got its second breath. Materially, the most extravagant dreams of the optimists had been more than realised; there had been no revolution; and, even if the national cake still failed to provide every British worker with all that he wanted, yet there seemed little reason to believe that this happy state was not round a nearby corner.

There is no particular reason to link these two developments of the 1880's—the growth of British mountaineering and the decrease in importance of those spiritual problems that epitomised the Victorian hey-day. There is no reason to believe that the British hills gave something less necessary than that exultation given by the Alps to Frederic Harrison when he wrote in praise of Alpine climbing: "We need sometimes that poetry should be not droned into our ears, but flashed into our senses." Yet it is a fact that the problems decreased; and that, simultaneously, those men who might have been driven to the Alps did find in the British hills some satisfaction similar to that which the earlier climbers had found in the Alps and in such greater ranges as they later visited.

Typical of the transition period during which the rambles of the fell-walkers were being replaced by the more ambitious adventures of the experienced Alpinists, was John Wilson Robinson, a dour Keswick estate agent, the son of a great fell-walker who had sketched the Napes Needle as early as 1828.

Robinson himself did not start climbing until 1882, when he made his first ascent of the Pillar, and it was about the same year that he first met Haskett-Smith, the young lawyer who played the most important part of all in the development of climbing in Britain during the latter quarter of the last century.

To the combination, Robinson brought his great local knowledge, gained not only during his walks on the fells, but during the day-to-day routine of his business. Even when one considers his luck in living so close to the hills, and his vigour—he once walked over the principal summits of the Lakes, a total of seventy miles, in twenty-four hours—the amount of climbing that he accomplished was astonishing. He ascended the Pillar 101 times between 1882 and 1906, taking between thirty and forty ladies to the top during this period, and also made more than fifty ascents of Scawfell Pinnacle, while between 1877 and 1903 he made nearly forty ascents of Great Gable.

Just as Coolidge was uninterested in any range other than the Alps, so was Robinson completely disinterested in the Alps or any other range outside Britain. He made one visit to the Alps, climbed the Matterhorn, which impressed him in a routine way, and thereafter concentrated solely on climbing in Britain.

Robinson's most constant companion in Britain was W. P. Haskett-Smith, "the father of British mountaineering", a man for whom the Alps and the Pyrenees, the latter of which he knew well, were but faint shadows of his own well-loved Lakeland fells.

Haskett-Smith stares from the portrait of the early climbing days slightly quizzically and rather defiantly, two attitudes which combined with his phenomenal list of first ascents to give him such a place in the story of British climbing. Born in 1859, he had a neat trim record typical of the times—Eton, Trinity, and Lincoln's Inn. Thereafter he departed from the conventions. He did not practise at the Bar, and Winthrop Young says that his only serious quarrel was when a fellow-member of the Alpine Club, thinking he was bestowing a favour, sent him a brief. He interested himself in the more abstruse aspects of philology, pottered around in a genial way, and became, like Coolidge, one of those rare things, a legend in his own lifetime.

His first visit to the British mountains was in 1882 when he spent nine weeks at Wasdale Head in the Lakes, explored Deep Ghyll, made the first ascent of Pavey Ark Gully, found a new high-level traverse across the north face of Great Gable, and explored the whole area for climbable routes—without, it should be noted, having had any more experience of mountains or mountaineering than had been gained from a stroll through the Pyrenees with Charles Packe during the previous year.

In 1884 he returned to the Lakes and continued his explorations there as he was to do, year after year, until the turn of the century. "Of course", he adds in what is a revealing comment on the period, "no ropes or other illegitimate means were resorted to." He pioneered first ascents of Scawfell, on Great Gable, Doe Crag, on the Napes Ridges, and on most other areas of rock which are today laced with routes.

It is, however, with the Napes Needle, the slender and spectacular pillar of rock standing out from the Napes Ridges, that Haskett-Smith is most intimately connected. He has described in an early number of the *Journal of the Fell and Rock Climbing Club of Great Britain*, how he came to make the historic first ascent. He had seen the Needle first on a misty day in the early 1880's, "a slender pinnacle of rock, standing out against the background of cloud without a sign of any other rock near it, and appearing to shoot up for 200–300 ft."

It was not until 1886, however, that he found himself alone, and in the late afternoon, in the gap which separates the Needle from the ridges which rise up the face of the mountain behind it.

> My first care [Haskett-Smith wrote later] was to get two or three stones and test the flatness of the summit by seeing whether anything thrown up could be induced to lodge. If it did, that would be an indication of a moderately flat top, and would hold out hopes of the edge being found not too much rounded to afford a good grip for the fingers. Out of three missiles, one consented to stay, and thereby encouraged me to start, feeling as small as a mouse climbing a milestone.
>
> Between the upper and lower blocks, about five feet up, there is a ragged horizontal chink large enough to admit the toes, but the trouble is to raise the body without intermediate footholds. It seemed best to work up at the extreme right, where the corner

38 O. G. Jones climbing in Derbyshire

39 J. W. Robinson and George Seatree at a Camp near Sty Head

40 The "Stable-door Traverse" at Wastdale Head

41 W. P. Haskett-Smith in his early climbing days

projects a little, though the fact that you are hanging over the deep gap makes it a rather "nervy" proceeding. For anyone in a standing position at the corner it is easy to shuffle the feet sideways to the other end of the chink, where it is found that the side of the top block facing outwards is decidedly less vertical. Moreover at the foot of this side there appeared to my great joy a protuberance which, being covered with a lichenous growth, looked as if it might prove slippery, but was placed in the precise spot where it would be most useful in shortening the formidable stretch up to the top edge. Gently and cautiously transferring my weight, I reached up with my right hand and at last was able to feel the edge and prove it to be, not smooth and rounded as it might have been, but a flat and satisfactory grip. My first thought on reaching the top was one of regret that my friends should have missed by a few hours such a day's climbing, three new things and all good [he had just made the first ascent of the Ennerdale face of Great Gable and the first continuous descent of the Needle Ridge]; my next was one of wonder whether getting down again would not prove far more awkward than getting up.

Hanging by the hands, and feeling with the toes for the protuberance provided an anxious moment, but the rest went easily enough, though it must be confessed that it was an undoubted satisfaction to stand once more on solid ground below and look up at my handkerchief fluttering in the breeze.

The Needle was not climbed again for three years and then three ascents were made within a few months. A lady, Miss Koecher, climbed it in 1890, and a few months later an illustrated article on the Needle appeared in the *Pall Mall Gazette*.

The fame of the spectacular spire of rock, the most photogenic in the country, soon spread. Spooner, the well-known photographer in the Strand, displayed a photograph of it in his shop window, and it was here that it first illustrated to O. G. Jones, a typical specimen of the second generation of British climbers, the possibilities offered by British mountains and hills.

In 1890 Jones, a technical student in London at the time, had visited the Lakes on a walking-tour and climbed the Pillar with no more knowledge of mountaineering than could be gleaned from the pages of *Prior's Guide*, a chatty little book that broke new ground by giving its readers some indication of the area's rock features.

The following year, walking down the Strand in London, oppressed with the flatness of people and things in general as he puts it, Jones glanced in Spooner's window, and for the first time, saw the outline of the Needle. Bystanders, he noted, looked at the tiny figures of climbers in the photograph and passed the usual uninformed remarks. "That evening", adds Jones, "a copy of the Needle hung in my room; in a fortnight, Easter had come round and I found myself on the top of the pinnacle."

Such was a typical result of Haskett-Smith's discovery. The photograph of the Needle—which was itself later taken as the emblem of the Fell and Rock Climbing Club—became a symbol of the new adventures to be found not beyond the Channel but in Britain itself. Today there are seven "regular" routes up the Needle, but the magic of its outline still holds. Perhaps the most moving day in its history came in 1936 when Haskett-Smith, then seventy-four, made his anniversary ascent, being led up to the summit by Lord Chorley, then President of the Fell and Rock, before an admiring audience of many hundreds ranged around the Dress Circle, the rocky bay on the Napes from which the Needle stands out in all its apparent inaccessibility.

As Haskett-Smith sat down on the uppermost block, a voice from the crowd below urged him to "Tell us a story." "There is no other story. This is the top storey", he immediately shouted back, a typical response from a man who devoted much of his life to the curiosities of words, to outlandish facts, and to useless but interesting branches of knowledge.

He climbed in Scotland and Wales, in the Pyrenees, the Alps, Norway, Spain, the Rockies, and even the Andes, but all his enjoyment and all his important climbing was concentrated on the Lakes.

Haskett-Smith not only "created" climbing in Britain; he also took the first step in its popularisation, and he would be of importance in the gradual expansion of mountaineering towards the end of the century if he had done nothing more than write and have published the two slim red-backed volumes of *Climbing in the British Isles.*

When the first of Haskett-Smith's volumes appeared in 1894, climbers had been describing their Alpine exploits in print for nearly half a century. Ball's *Alpine Guide* was merely one of the short cuts to Alpinism that had been making the way even easier for young men wishing to take up climbing. It is true that there had been, as there still is, a feeling that the more reckless expeditions should not be given too bright a limelight; yet so far as the great majority of new expeditions and ascents were concerned they had been, since the early 1880's, recorded either in the *Alpine Journal* or in one of the many records of private exploration that were published, if privately, at least in sufficient numbers to fill the demand.

The position of British rock-climbing intelligence was a little different. Virtually no printed information had appeared in 1884 when two articles on the subject were published in *All the Year Round.* The first climbers' log-book had appeared at Wastdale Head only four years earlier. Haskett-Smith's were therefore the first to break the unwritten law that accounts of climbs in Britain should be passed down only by word of mouth so that information would be graded according to the experience of the recipient.

This state of affairs was a happy, but impermanent, one. "For some years past", said Haskett-Smith in his preface, "there has been a remarkably rapid increase in the number of men who climb for climbing's sake within the bounds of the British Isles." It was for them that the little red-bound books were intended, a primer for the embryonic mountaineers who might otherwise "have missed their vocation because they were in the position of the prudent individual who would not go into the water until after he had learned to swim".

Mere numbers alone are no index of the influence exerted by Haskett-Smith's guides after their quiet explosion on the Victorian scene. Between their publication and the mid-1930's, in fact, they sold only some 3,000 copies each, a striking comparison with the 120,000 copies of the late J. E. Q. Barford's *Climbing in*

Britain which were sold within a few years of its publication roughly half a century later. Yet it is not too much to claim that "Haskett-Smith" opened the floodgates which the pioneers had slowly begun to move. The volumes paved the way for O. G. Jones' more detailed *Climbing in the English Lake District*, for the lavishly illustrated volumes of the Abraham brothers and, ultimately, for the whole shelf-loads of detailed climbing-guides which today deal with the most minor routes up the most inconspicuous boulders. Some of these have continued the tradition of mild humour with which Haskett-Smith laced most of his descriptions; none have contained such a wealth of detail about the less technical but more human aspects of the sport.

The publication of "Haskett-Smith" underlined the fact that climbing in Britain now existed as a sport in its own right, as something distinct from, and not necessarily linked with, climbing in the Alps or elsewhere. It was a sport which grew enormously as the century drew to its close and which was different in two important ways from mountaineering as it had been thought of and practised during the previous half-century.

The relative nearness of the mountains to the climbers' homes had two major results. In the first place, the hills lost something of their mystery. The mountains at the end of the street could never be quite the same as the mountains which lay beyond the sea, in a foreign land where they still posed topographical problems even though the solution of these was no longer hindered by the presence of dragons.

Almost as important was the fact that climbers living so relatively close to the mountains could, by constant practise, achieve a proficiency impossible for those whose climbing was limited to a few weeks or perhaps months every year. Thus the climbers on British hills towards the end of the century began, on rocks at least, to approach that technical efficiency which had previously been the prerogative of the Alpine guide.

By the turn of the century mountaineering in Britain, the off-shoot of Victorian Alpinism, had grown into a lusty plant.

An off-shoot it was, however. Many of the basic factors which brought about the growth of mountaineering in the fifties and sixties still existed. Their presence, grim and challenging, is shown most clearly by that epitome of all later Victorians, Martin Conway, later Lord Conway of Allington.

Chapter Ten

CONWAY, THE VICTORIAN MOUNTAINEER

From too much love of living,
From fear and hope set free,
We thank with brief thanksgiving
Whatever Gods may be
That no life lives for ever;
That dead men rise up never;
That even the weariest river
Winds somewhere safe to sea.

SWINBURNE

AMONG the mountaineers and mountain-lovers of the nineteenth century there had been many for whom the beauty of the heights had been one of the main, if one of the most elusive, attractions offered by the Alps. Ruskin had been the most prominent of them but there had also been Elizah Walton, E. T. Coleman, George Barnard, and H. G. Willink. Yet it was not until Conway arrived upon the scene with the full flourish of a connoisseur's knowledge that an active mountaineer, well versed in the craft, with all the minutiae of the sport at his finger-tips, and in his pocket the money to indulge it, was to approach the Alps with what was basically an artist's outlook.

Just as the earlier mountaineers had subordinated all else to the process of getting their instruments in the right place at the right time—creating only incidentally the craft of travel above the snowline—so did Conway plan much of his mountaineering life in order that the exquisite mountain view, the panorama seen, as the pioneers had seen it, with eyes of wonder, the unique ridge viewed end-on with peculiar perspective, should separately or together form a part of each day's journeying. From his writings there comes the same impression; the feeling that an important part of each expedition was in fact a search for some new facet of the Alpine world which could be viewed with the eyes not only of the climber but of the artist. There is nothing quite like it, and few things so good, in the whole of Alpine literature.

There were many factors which combined to ease William Martin Conway, later Lord Conway of Allington, into the enviable position which he enjoyed throughout the last quarter of the nineteenth century. Born in 1856, he came of age after the first great mountain problems had been solved; he could, therefore, devote himself to those in which history, topography, or art, as well as pure conquest, played their respective parts. He was lucky in his parents, and in his position in life, and it is easy to claim that the more obviously inherited features of his life were responsible for his success. This is not entirely true.

It would be fair to say that everything Conway touched turned, if not to gold yet at least to a not unprofitable venture. It is true that he can have seen little financial profit from some of his larger expeditions, but he had a background to cushion him against such occasional and minor matters. There were few amateurs of the period who could plan, as Conway planned, to employ another amateur—the late Oscar Eckenstein—as a professional guide on a lengthy journey to India. He could write, with no offence, of "my artist", A. D. MacCormick, who accompanied him to the Himalayas and illustrated a number of his books. His planning of an expedition to the most distant ranges of the world was usually a question not of money but of time; and when his plan for a whole series of climbing guides had been rejected by the Alpine Club he was quite prepared to embark on the task himself, virtually underwriting whatever loss might ensue. It was perhaps significant that when, as a child, he reached the top of Snowdon for the first time and found himself too small to add a stone to the cairn, his cousin's butler did so for him.

Yet happy financial circumstances would have been nothing without the man himself. And, of all the Victorian mountaineers,

Martin Conway most nearly approached the Elizabethan ideal of the "compleat man". His mind was the equal of his six-foot stature: his humility to the confidence with which he would tackle the most difficult or abstruse Alpine problem. An almost medieval chivalry and other-worldliness appeared to govern his life, and it was natural that in the untrodden mountains of distant ranges he should see some challenge to the explainable facts of life.

So far as mountains were concerned he was the incurable Romantic, and it is not too much to claim that they ruled his life just as surely as they ruled that of the Alpine guide.

> Wide outspreading vistas, thank heaven, still retain for me the same mysterious charm that belonged to that one [he wrote some sixty years after having first seen the view from the Malvern Beacon]. The delusion that somewhere, far off in the blue distance, lurks the Perfect Place, that the blue hills really are blue, that what one beholds is in its essence actually as beautiful as from above it seems—so long as that delusion lasts, Romance lingers.

And, like most of the Victorian climbers, he was tough. It is "the cold air" which is "laden with the very spirit of romance". He goes neither carefully nor cautiously and can write with real relief of finding himself after some escapade as "suddenly in the world of living people with a future to look forward to as well as a past to remember".

Almost every aspect of the mountain world interested him. One of the most important, an aspect which appears surprising to anyone surveying the whole man, was the study of mountain history and topography that by the later seventies was beginning to draw poor Coolidge ever more surely and irretrievably into its clutches. Conway, however, always kept history in its place as a servant.

He had made the ascent of the Breithorn in 1872, at the age of sixteen but it was only in 1876, when he first visited the Engadine, that his serious climbing started. Thereafter, he returned to the Alps year after year, climbing frequently either with George Scriven, an Irish doctor whom he had known as a boy at Repton, or with Penhall who was later killed on the Wetterhorn.

42 The Spring Meet of the Cairngorm Club on Mount Keen, 1890

New routes up previously climbed mountains were the order of the day, and it was here that Conway, like many others, ran into difficulties. A hard day's work among the journals of the various European Alpine Clubs was often needed to ensure that a proposed "new" route had not, in fact, been climbed and recorded in some obscure publication; even such checking and cross-checking might not be conclusive. After two seasons at Zermatt with Scriven, Conway records that "only once did we venture on a new way up Monte Rosa, which to our disgust afterwards proved to be not new but only unrecorded". It was an error that Conway did not intend to repeat. He was then at Trinity and on his return from the Alps set to work in the University Library, intent on providing, at his own publishing cost if need be, a handy volume which would save climbers from similar errors in the future.

He was only half-certain of the need for the book. He was only twenty-four. He had been a member of the Alpine Club for only three years, and it was natural that he would ask advice from Coolidge, six years his senior and the newly appointed editor of the *Alpine Journal*.

His first letter to Coolidge, the vanguard of many hundreds which were to pass between the two men during the next half-century, summed up his doubts.

> I have recently been constructing a small pocket-book for mountaineers dealing with the Zermatt mountains [he said]. Do you think that such a commodity is wanted? and do you approve of the proposed flap-pocket-book form? It appears that the cost of publication of 500 copies would be £50, do you imagine that 500 people would turn up—say in the next five years—to whom such a book would be a boon?

Coolidge lived for such requests. By return there went to Conway a four-point list of comments, suggestions, a "liberal order of copies", and an offer to read the proofs. As a result there appeared in 1881 the record of ascents around Zermatt, replete with a fine fund of historical information, all presented, in the flap-pocket-book form, for a single half-crown—the *Zermatt*

Pocket-Book, that ancestor of all the dozens of little volumes in whose pages one may today find the faces of the Alps cross-hatched with routes, sub-routes, and demi-semi sub-routes. Even at *2s. 6d.*, sales lagged. Four years after publication, more than 100 copies still remained in the hands of the publishers, although when these had finally gone the second-hand price of the book rose swiftly.

> When the price of it rose to a pound, and I had acquired a great deal of information, I decided to print a new edition [Conway later wrote]. That was issued in two parts, an East half and a West. As I explained in the preface, that was done to make it necessary for any climber to buy both parts. Moreover, as they had been willing to pay a pound for a second-hand first edition, I decided that they should pay me the same price for a much better and fuller book, and they did.

The comment, typical as it is of the worldly-wise façade which Conway habitually erected, does him less than justice. His letters to Coolidge, hundred upon hundred of them, their writing sandwiched between work as a prospective M.P., studies as a rising art connoisseur, and a whole wealth of public and private duties ("This is my 40th letter today", he says in the pre-type-writer days. "I am nearly killed with piled-up details"), reflect far more accurately the reasons for his continuing interest in the guide. "The easy approaches of ecstatic enthusiasm were passed", he explains. "The region of serious investigation and study had now to be traversed." The continuing enquiry into Alpine history was part of the traverse. Publication of the results was, if nothing else, part of a scholar's duty.

The *Zermatt Pocket-Book*, however, was only a beginning. When preparing for its reissue, Conway had proposed to the Alpine Club that they should allow him to publish it "as the first part of an A.C. Guide to the High Alps". The Club, probably with an eye on the republication of "Ball", rejected the scheme. Conway mulled over the idea with Coolidge and between them they built up the skeleton of the series on which they subsequently worked for years and which was published as the Conway and Coolidge's Climbers' Guides. Only a publisher was lacking.

T. Fisher Unwin, after suitable preparation by Conway, was agreeable but cautious, as well as worried by the possible length, unreadability, and general unmanageability of what might be prepared in the way of copy. Coolidge's reputation had gone before him.

Conway, anxious that the first contact between Unwin and Coolidge should take place with as little argument as possible, warned and advised his collaborator, in a letter marked "very particularly and extremely and altogether especially private", of the line that could best be taken.

> Let TFU down lightly [he advised]. Don't threaten him, but just send him your MS and he'll take it all right, especially if you send him the short Lepontine Vol. first. Say you have borrowed a few pages from that to add to the other—as soon as he has put his money into a volume or two *we hold him.* Don't forewarn him of prospective troubles, and in case of a longer volume than usual, let him have the first part of the MS first and let that *be in type before he sees the last part* or knows how long it will be. It's only a question of management; if things get stiff at any time I will ask TFU to lunch at the Savile, for election to which he is a candidate.

As a gentle exercise in the art of twisting the arm, it was a beautiful example, typical of the operation, extending over many years, which was to give the Alpine world the volumes of the Conway-Coolidge guides.

The story of the guides is in some ways a minor saga—of pedantic but academically justified argument on Coolidge's part, of sweet reasonableness on Conway's. It was Conway who finally had Coolidge's "honorarium" of five pounds per volume doubled. It was Conway, "the buffer in the matter" as he describes himself, who smoothed out the ferocious argument that arose when Unwin proposed that one of Coolidge's unwieldy, over-annotated volumes should be split into two. Coolidge, breathing blood and fire, was all for claiming that such a move would break the publishing agreement and lay the way open for legal action. Conway acted as mediator, pointed out that Unwin could not do the economically impossible, and finally persuaded Coolidge to agree. Few men, incidentally, can have so little justified Coolidge's idea of a grasping publisher as did Unwin. "I doubt if the publication of these volumes will ever repay me", he wrote of another publishing proposal for mountain books, "and yet I love the mountains so well that I am much interested in them."

An astonishing amount of time, thought, and undiluted brain-sweat was lavished on the Conway-Coolidge guides. The hundreds of letters dealing with each volume that passed between the two men during the period of genesis form an indication of just how much work was involved.

By the early nineties, however, Conway had already begun to realise that while the mountains might satisfy all manner of demands, the Alps themselves suggested something better in the greater ranges beyond Europe. Short travels in Egypt, Syria, Cyprus, Greece, and Turkey had awakened what even in later life he called the romance of the East.

> I found it wonderful [he says] to be in the midst of a people not ashamed to acknowledge God by publicly praying wherever they happened to be at the hour of prayer, and performing their devotions in those monumental attitudes wherewith Islam has endowed the world.

Back in Britain, he was restless and dissatisfied, uneasy with a desire that not all the excitement of his expanding public life could fully satisfy. The outcome was his first great tour of exploration, a journey that was to take him and his companions higher than man had ever been before, deep into the heart of the Karakoram, among the greatest glaciers of the world.

The plan had been roughly formed in 1890 and had matured during the following year. Freshfield and Mummery, it was at first intended, were to accompany Conway. Freshfield was forced by circumstances to withdraw, while Conway and Mummery realised, after a friendly pilot-run in the Graians, that their ideas of mountain-climbing were so different as to preclude any likelihood of ideal co-operation on a major enterprise. It was a sensible decision and later events proved that a similar trial between Conway and Oscar Eckenstein, who had been asked to join the party and who was to have come in a semi-professional capacity—might have proved equally useful. As it was, difficulties arose with Eckenstein, that queer friend of Aleister Crowley; and, as Conway says in his sole reference to Eckenstein in the lengthy record of the expedition which he subsequently wrote, "he did not come with me beyond Nagar", a point at which the expedition had not truly begun.

With him, on this journey to the Karakoram, Conway brought A. D. MacCormick, the artist of the expedition, and Lt. Bruce, one of the first men to believe that Everest could be climbed, and as General Bruce the leader of the first full-scale expedition to Everest in 1922. As guide, Conway had Matthias Zurbruggen of Macugnaga of whom he later wrote:

> He was by nature ambitious of attainment. He desired to acquire every sort of knowledge and every sort of skill that he could come by. Ultimately, he could speak English, French, German, Italian, a little Spanish and (when in India), a smattering of Hindustani. He was also a competent blacksmith, a good carpenter, a useful all round man with his hands, and a most accomplished craftsman with axe and rope on the mountain-side. . . . He was everlastingly picking up information of one kind and another. I never knew a man with a more hospitable mind, nor one better gifted by nature with the potentialities of scholarship.

In his own more rough-hewn way he must have been uncommonly like Conway himself.

The Royal Geographical Society, the Royal Society, and the British Association, all contributed to the costs of the expedition which as Conway ruefully admitted later were considerably greater than had been expected. "Experience", he commented on his return, "had to be purchased. Mine is at the service of any future traveller who chooses to apply for it."

The experience was considerable, for the expedition, in which Conway was not only leader and organiser, but leading climber, leading surveyor, and half a hundred other things, succeeded in carrying out the first major reconnaissance of a great Asian glacier. "What Freshfield did for the Caucasus, Conway did for the Himalaya", it has been said. "He was the man who brought the Himalaya to Europe."

He surveyed the Hispar and Baltoro Glaciers. He unravelled the intimate topography of a great knot of high mountains that had not before been seen by Europeans. He reached the summit of the 23,000-ft. Pioneer Peak, then the greatest height attained by man. He won a knighthood for the work. He came back to Britain perhaps more profoundly dissatisfied than ever, so near had he been to finding what he sought.

> Romance almost became a reality [he writes of his experiences in the great Biafo Valley]. The gods were very near at hand. We touched as it were the skirts of their garments. Yet even at the culminating moments of these strenuous dream-days there still lingered the sense of incompleteness, of something lacking. The secret was almost disclosed, but never quite, the veil never entirely withdrawn.

Back in Britain he took up the threads dropped by the successful young man of independent means. He remained unsatisfied. The restlessness grew throughout the months, and in 1894 he embarked on a minor dream which had occupied many of his thoughts throughout the long years of Alpine research with Coolidge—his traverse of the "Alps from End to End".

Conway had been, for many years, a violent and sometimes unpopular protagonist of the ex-centrist theory of Alpinism. He did not believe that a man should settle down comfortably in an Alpine hotel and then climb all the peaks within range. Climbing was something different and more spiritually adventurous than this for Conway. Every day had to mount up to a new prospect for the morrow. Every day had to see not only an accomplishment, but a new, opening-out vista whose prospect had lain unrevealed until the last possible moment. It was an almost revolutionary idea, and certainly a good one in an age when the Alps were, in the recurrent phrase, "played out".

In pursuing it, Conway had more than once tried to press on to a reluctant Alpine Club his idea of a small select band, a club within a club, an idea which he had once propounded to Coolidge.

> I am going to read the Xmas paper to A.C. [he said]. I don't know about what, but I shall bring in my "Alpine Wanderers' Section of the A.C." proposal. To this end, I want the Alps divided into groups, and no man should be allowed to join the A. Wanderers who had not climbed at least one mountain and crossed one pass in at least one-quarter of the groups, and no one sd. be a life-member who had not dittoed in at least $\frac{3}{4}$—others to cease to be members after three non-wandering seasons. A peak to be at least 3,000m, a pass 2,500m unless special reasons for admitting a lower one.
>
> No life-member to be able to qualify with less than 6 years of wandering. The division into groups is not for scientific purposes but intended to spread a man's travels. The area of each group should be traversed from end to end, a mere run into the edge of a group and out again must not count.

Conway had divided the Alps into nearly thirty groups, and through virtually all of them he passed during the journey he began in the summer of 1894, and during which he was to climb twenty-one peaks and thirty-nine passes with Zurbruggen, two of the Ghurkas who had been with him in the Himalayas, and a young climber called Edward Fitzgerald who accompanied the party sporadically with his two guides.

Conway had had great ideas for Fitzgerald.

> I have long thought [he wrote to Coolidge in 1893] that it would be a good thing to get a young member of the Club into training as an Alpine literature expert. I think I have found the man—Edward Fitzgerald. He is aged 22, newly married, a keen collector and reader of Alpine books, has done several years climbing, is a man of means and leisure, and wants to do something. . . . I mean to make him a kind of sub-editor of the "Alpine Journal" [he was then in charge of the *Journal*], to receive and answer letters, etc. I shall make him go and call on you at Oxford when you come home and you will then be able to instill into him scholarly notions, and see what you think of him. He is a very retiring, solitary person, and might grow into a good editor if properly trained from the start.

The suggestion was typical of Conway's good nature, of his feeling for Alpine history, and of the careful way in which he organised all his affairs. For Fitzgerald, it was a great opportunity. He dropped it with both hands.

Conway's journey took him from the Col di Tenda at the western end of the Alps to Monte Viso, Mont Blanc, the Nord-end of Monte Rosa, the Jungfrau, the first ascent and passage of what Conway gallantly named the Piz Ghurka and the Gurkha Pass, and into Austria and the Gross Glockner and the Ankogel.

He returned to Britain, partially satisfied at least, unsuccessfully contested Bath, and might well have been expected to settle down in enjoyment of his reputation. He had been knighted as a result of his Himalayan journey; he had a growing reputation as an art connoisseur; he was the author of four books which had brought him, if no great financial reward, at least an enviable renown.

He was nearly forty. It might, his friends must have felt, have been a wise thing to consolidate, to let the unknown rest in its obscurity. Conway was not that sort of man.

> I have never sought to be wise [he wrote later], but always to plunge into the unknown, to get away from the dull round of everyday and go forth as student or adventurer into subjects or regions where it seems to me at the moment that the unattained might be attainable, the unexperienced might be felt.

It was in this mood that he received a short contribution for the *Alpine Journal* dealing with Spitzbergen. For most people there was little lustre or romance or opportunity about the place. For Conway, the unexpected article pointed the way. Perhaps Spitzbergen might provide a different set of sensations, a different collection of landscapes. Perhaps it might even be a country where, in close contact with land, sea, and water, he might find the answer to those problems which he was still seeking. He continued to think of Spitzbergen. Then the vague ideas were suddenly crystallised.

> Early one morning [he says] I was riding along the bank of the Serpentine in Hyde Park. It was misty and the water had been

44 A Group on Cader Idris in 1897

45 Lord Conway of Allington

frozen over. The sheet of ice was broken up and the sun was penetrating the mist and glittering on the ice. The tender evanescent beauty of the scene took sudden possession of me. Thus, perhaps, on a grander scale, might arctic visions fashion themselves. At that moment the fates decided for me the two expeditions carried out in 1896 and 1897.

On the first of these, Conway made the pioneer crossing of Spitzbergen; on the second he made the first ascent of a number of peaks; on both he added immeasurably to the knowledge of a virtually unknown and unmapped country one-third the size of the whole British Isles. He did more than add to knowledge, however. Conway had the facility for recording and interpreting his knowledge so that it was readily understandable to the non-technical mind; he had a unique facility for taking descriptive writing to the nearest possible fringe of the purple patch; and he had an enthusiasm for all that he did that bubbled over into his writing. In one important way, he differed from most of the other climbers of his period; he evinced no wish to convert. He was not, like most of them, trying to exhort his readers up into the mountains. Reading Conway one has the impression of a man entranced with all that he saw and translating the vision, almost by accident, into such a form that all other men might understand it.

There is his description of an evening when the final crossing of Spitzbergen was still in the balance.

Climbing the hill above camp the moment it was pitched, I rose above the ice-wall which proved to be the side of the snout of a great glacier [he says]. When at last I could look over it and beyond —lo! the eastern sea with Edge Island rising out of it and the ice-pack stretching away to a remote and clear horizon. I yelled down to my friends in camp, then climbed higher and higher and saw to even greater distances. Aghard Bay just beyond the glacier was sparkling in sunlight and dotted over with speckles and streaks of ice. The water was blue; blue, too, were the hills of Edge Island, and presently purple; the remotest of them ablaze with yellow light. Up and up I went, leaning against a gale till all the nearer hills were disclosed, domes of snow from which the big glacier descended. The limb of a rainbow was standing upon the ice. It was a view not merely worth seeing, but well worth having come to see.

As a specimen of prose it is typical of Conway, the master, it seems, of almost everything to which he turned his hand. That he did turn his hand to innumerable subjects is shown by the record after his return from Spitzbergen, for he had become, it was soon shown, an expert on half a dozen aspects of the island and its history.

The following summer he was off again, this time to South America, on a long, rambling journey, rather more expensive than usual, one must imagine, during which he made the first ascent of Illimani and an ascent of Aconcagua.

The account of what happened on Aconcagua shows, better than most incidents, the type of man that Conway was. Fitzgerald, the young man of whom Conway had had great hopes, had himself been on the mountain the previous year while Conway was in Spitzbergen—using, incidentally, Matthias Zurbruggen, Conway's former guide—and was generally believed to have reached the top. When, therefore, Conway reached the final ridge after infinite trouble, labour, and not a little danger, he halted.

> Fitzgerald's book had not been published at the time of my ascent [he explained later]. I thought, and I believe correctly, that it would be harmful for the prestige of that book, just at the point of issue, if I were known to have accomplished in a week that was supposed to have taken Fitzgerald's party several months.

It was only later that Conway learned that Fitzgerald, who apparently had not taken his training seriously enough, had broken down on the upper slopes of the mountain and had allowed his first ascent to be made by his guide.

From Aconcagua, Conway returned to Valparaiso, then travelled south to Tierra del Fuego, wandering almost discontentedly; maybe "in search of the Divine" as he called his last book.

He returned to Britain early in 1899 and two years later took his official farewell to mountaineering by ascending the Breithorn with his daughter. It was her first climb, as it had been his some twenty-nine years earlier. There was a certain formalised, almost artificial ending to his association with active mountaineering. He was just forty-seven.

Conway was to fill illustrious positions in the Royal Geographical Society; he was to become President of the Alpine Club—and of the Ligue pour la Conservation de la Suisse pittoresque which fought the Matterhorn railway scheme. He was to become an important figure, a link with the mountaineering past, born before the formation of the Alpine Club. He outlived Coolidge, and Freshfield, and when his death came in 1937 he was the last survivor of the heroic age. Yet after the age of forty-seven his only climbs were those on a few holiday peaks.

The explanation is more simple than one might at first imagine. For Conway, the mountains had performed their function; they had served the purpose for which he believed them to exist. Conway had gone to the mountains for the same reason that most other Victorian climbers had, to a lesser or greater degree, gone to them. He had gone to discover some indication that man was something more than the six-foot body that contained him, to discover whether or not he formed an essential part of an understandable universe. For Conway, seeking more carefully, probing more deeply, than some of the others, the experiences of the mountains had proved that there were, after all, gods in spite of the scientists. There was still some doubt as to who they were, and Conway sought new methods of investigation.

> Each book of life that in turn we open we must one day close [he explained]. All save the last, which we shall be called from half-read. For all of us there are many kinds of joy as yet unexperienced, many activities untried, many fields of knowledge unexplored. We must not spend too large a fraction of life over one or the next will escape us. It is life, after all, that is the greatest field of exploration.

Here, for Conway as for so many of his companions, was the

real glory; that, half conquerors, half pilgrims, they were able to stride into the darkness with a confidence found in the Alps, hoping that they yet might find some all-embracing belief that had eluded both them and the age through which they had thundered.

INDEX

The numerals in **heavy** type denote the *figure numbers* of the illustrations